Saxo Grammaticus

A Medieval Author
between Norse and Latin Culture

University of
1479

Copenhagen
1979

Danish Medieval History & Saxo Grammaticus
A symposium held in celebration of the
500th anniversary of
the University of Copenhagen

Volume II

SAXO GRAMMATICUS

A MEDIEVAL AUTHOR
BETWEEN NORSE AND LATIN
CULTURE

Edited by
Karsten Friis-Jensen

MUSEUM TUSCULANUM PRESS
COPENHAGEN 1981

© Museum Tusculanum Press 1981
Cover: Bent Kvisgaard
Printed in Special-Trykkeriet Viborg a-s
ISBN: 87-88073-32-7

ACKNOWLEDGEMENTS

On the occasion of the 500th anniversary of *Københavns Universitet* the University Senate invited the Faculty of Arts to arrange a number of symposia in celebration of the event. Subjects were to be chosen in which the university could claim to maintain significant scholarly traditions. The faculty acknowledged DANISH MEDIEVAL HISTORY and SAXO GRAMMATICUS as such subjects and suggested that they be combined into one symposium. The President of the University, Professor Morten Lange, recommended this plan.

In September 1979 the plan was realized thanks to generous grants from *Augustinus Fonden, Krista og Viggo Petersens Fond, A.P. Møller og Hustru Chastine Mc-Kinney-Møllers Fond til almene Formål, Carlsbergs Mindefond for Brygger J.C. Jacobsen,* and *Dansk-Finsk Fond, Dansk-Islandsk Fond* and *Fonden for dansk-svensk Samarbejde.* We offer our warmest thanks to these foundations. Grants towards the cost of publication of the present two volumes of proceedings have also been received from the Danish Research Council for the Humanities and from the Faculty of Arts of the University, and the committee takes great pleasure in expressing its gratitude for this support. It also wishes to thank Professors Johnny Christensen and Jan Pinborg and Mr. Ivan Boserup for their active help in planning the symposium.

We were fortunate to be able to hold the symposium at *Det Kongelige Danske Videnskabernes Selskab,* and we thank its presidium and staff for their hospitality.

It is also a pleasure to thank the secretarial staff of the departments of history and classics for the prompt assistance rendered by them in all phases of the work, as well as Mr. H.A. Hens, who gave excellent help in recording the papers and discussions, and Miss Hanne Lassen, who assisted us both before and during the symposium.

Niels Skyum-Nielsen   Karsten Friis-Jensen   Niels Lund

EDITOR'S NOTE

All the papers read at the Saxo section of the symposium are printed in the present volume, together with Joaquín Martínez-Pizarro's paper from the Fourth International Saga Conference in Munich (1979) on Saxo's *Ericus Disertus*. In addition Birgit Strand has expanded her remarks at the symposium on *Thyra Danebod*. Especially in connection with the Saxo section I wish to thank our excellent chairman, Dr. Jørgen Raasted; Peter Fisher, who undertook to remove the most conspicuous solecisms in the contributions from us Scandinavians; and Marianne Pade for her assistance with the preparation of this volume for publication. I am also grateful to Oxford University Press for permission to quote in my own paper from Gordon Williams's translation of Book III of Horace's Odes.

Karsten Friis-Jensen

CONTENTS

THE ANGERS FRAGMENT AND THE ARCHETYPE
OF GESTA DANORUM

IVAN BOSERUP

Royal Library, Copenhagen

Except for some indirect and not very reliable evidence, and for five fragments of medieval manuscripts amounting, when taken together, to a few pages of text, our only witness to the text of Saxo's Gesta Danorum is the editio princeps, printed in Paris in 1514. The purpose of this paper is to discuss whether the archetype of the editio princeps was written by Saxo himself, or, as commonly claimed, our text is interpolated, being the product of a 13th century editor working on a draft left unfinished by Saxo. I shall first summarize the history of the problem together with a presentation and brief discussion of the witnesses to Saxo's text; then I shall suggest some new evidence to the effect that our text is not based on an interpolated archetype. The stemma codicum and sigla below will serve for easy reference; the stemma corresponds to modern consensus, and will not be discussed in detail.

Christiern Pedersen

Saxo's voluminous work in sixteen books was epitomized in the middle of the 14th century (**j**), and a Low German translation of the epitome was printed by Matthæus Brandis about 1502. But the original version was not forgotten: in a Latin grammar printed in Copenhagen in 1493 for the use of students at the university, the reason given for learning prosody and metre is that it is a necessary condition for the correct understanding of the verses of "Boethius, Saxo Grammaticus, and other authors"[1]. Hence, when the bishop of Roskilde Lage Urne urged the young Danish humanist Christiern Pedersen (ca. 1480-1554), then studying in Paris, to produce an edition of Saxo, it was due to the fact that the rise of learning in Denmark in the late 15th century created an increased demand for

Stemma:

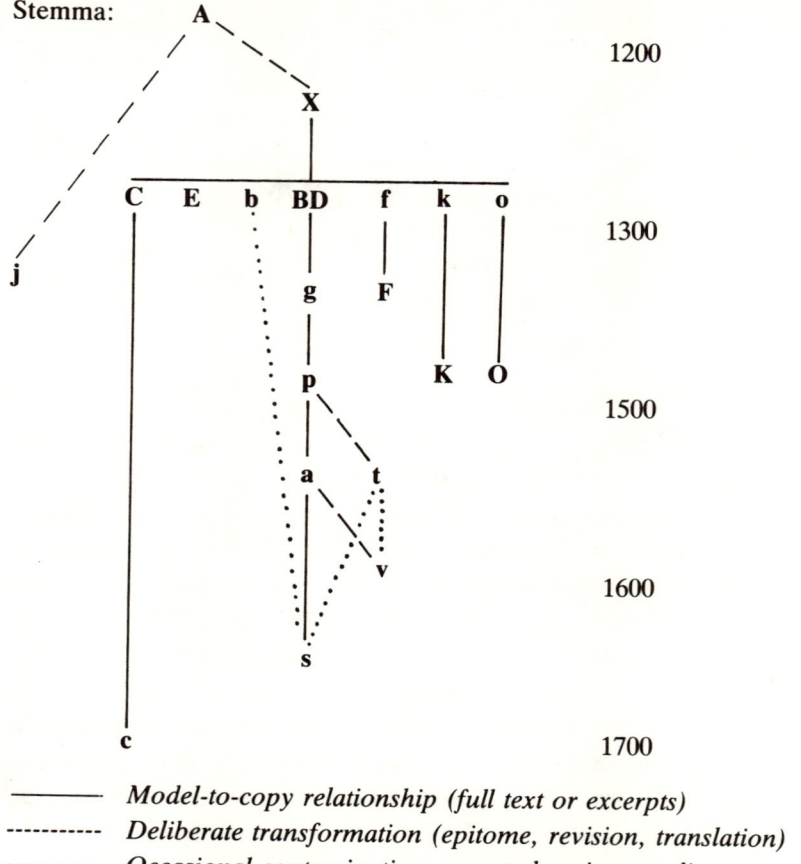

1200
1300
1500
1600
1700

——————— *Model-to-copy relationship (full text or excerpts)*
----------- *Deliberate transformation (epitome, revision, translation)*
··········· *Occasional contamination, reported variant readings*

Sigla:

A	Angers fragment
a	Paris edition, 1514
BD	Lassen + Kall-Rasmussen's fragments
b	Codex of Caspar Barth (lost)
C	Laverentzen's fragment (lost)
c	Collation of C
E	Plesner's fragment
F	Chronicon Sialandiae
f	Codex used by **F** (lost)
g	Codex of Birger Gunnersen (lost)

j	Compendium Saxonis
K	Albert Krantz
k	Codex used by **K** (lost)
O	Peder Olsen
o	Codex used by **O** (lost)
p	Copy of **g** used for printing **a** (lost)
s	Stephanius' Saxo edition and commentary, 1645
t	Christiern Pedersen's translation (lost)
v	A. S. Vedel's translation, 1575
x	Archetype of the medieval vulgate (lost)

copies of Gesta Danorum, without comparison the most important literary monument to the glorious past of the Danes.

In the three laudatory letters prefixed to the editio princeps and serving as a kind of foreword, Lage Urne mentions the great admiration felt for Saxo by »all learned and renowned men«, and Christiern Pedersen states that the main difficulty was not that he could find no manuscript upon which to base his edition, but the fact that no one in Denmark would sell or lend him such a treasure as a Saxo codex, no matter how old and damaged; true, a professor at the university volonteered to copy a manuscript for him, but Christiern Pedersen declined this magnificent offer; at last, however, the archbishop of Lund Birger Gunnersen found a codex (**g**) that could be taken to Paris to be "transcribed and printed".

Christiern Pedersen's edition (**a**), apparently based on a copy (**p**) of **g**, was printed "in inclyta Parrhisiorum academia" on March 15th 1514 by Jodocus Badius Ascensius, professor at the Sorbonne and famous editor and commentator of numerous classical Latin texts. The edition proudly presents itself as printed "with the utmost care", but it does in fact contain quite a number of misprints[2].

Christiern Pedersen also made a Danish translation of Saxo (**t**), apparently based on **p** (or **g**), not on **a**, but it was destroyed when the University Library burned down in the great fire of Copenhagen in 1728. However, Anders Sørensen Vedel (1542-1616) had access to it when he made his Danish translation of Saxo[3], printed 1575 (**v**), and Stephanius quotes one long and a few shorter passages from **t** in his Notæ uberiores (1645) (**s**). Indirectly, therefore, **s** and **v** are of some help when we try to assess **a**'s adherence to the tradition upon which it is based.

Stephanius

The text of the editio princeps (**a**) was reissued in Basel 1534 and in Frankfurt 1576, but with the exception of Vedel, who writes in his foreword that in the translation he has corrected more than one hundred of **a**'s misprints[4], no serious critical work on Saxo seems to have been done until the Danish scholar Stephanus Johannis Stephanius (1599-1650) set out to prepare a new edition together with a full philological and exegetical commentary.

Stephanius made inquiries in Scandinavian libraries and among learned colleagues about medieval manuscripts of Saxo, but without success. Few medieval manuscripts survived the turmoils of the Reformation period in Denmark, and the last known complete codex of Saxo (**b**) burned in 1633 – if we are to believe the German scholar Caspar Barth, as famous for his "disregard for veracity"[5] as for his encyclopedic knowledge. In the prolegomena to the Notæ uberiores, Stephanius quotes a letter from Barth telling about the destruction of most of his library, including his codex of Saxo (with marginalia) and two copies of it. Before the catastrophe, however, Stephanius had obtained from Barth a modest number of variant readings from this codex, often supplemented with Barth's own conjectures. Caspar Barth was a famous man during his lifetime, and Stephanius expresses great respect for him, but he rejects most of the readings and conjectures of which Barth was so proud[6], and one may well doubt whether Stephanius believed that Barth's codex would have helped him to produce a fundamentally more sound text of Saxo. All things considered, **b** testifies to the high quality of **a** and its tradition.

With no access to medieval manuscripts, Stephanius was obliged to base his text on **a** alone, – and on his critical judgement. He had early started work on Saxo[7], and his new edition with a commentary was ready many years before it was printed[8]. While he waited for the necessary grants, he published the two short historical works of Sven Aggesen, Saxo's "contubernalis", from a manuscript in the University Library in Copenhagen (1642). Contrary to Saxo, this author writes in quite ordinary medieval Latin, and Stephanius did not hesitate to rewrite the text in a more classical idiom in order to make it more elevated and readable[9]: during his years of study at Leiden he had learnt to distinguish correct Latin from incorrect Latin by close empirical scrutiny of classical Latin authors[10]. However, if Stephanius was radical in his critical and stylistic approach to ordinary medieval texts, he was all the more cautious when working on the classicizing Latin of Saxo Grammaticus. Obviously, he considered the transmitted text to be coherent and reliable, and he solved the problems he encountered not by expunging words, interpolating sentences, or moving whole chapters around, but by means of a sustained exegetical effort, and, when no other solution was at hand, by isolating and correcting small mistakes made by copyists or by the printer. This general approach is characteristic of Stephanius' first contribution to Saxo scholarship from 1627, and even more so of his monumental edition from 1645. Over the years, he had become more familiar with Saxo's Latin, and in 1645 he withdrew or passed over in silence a number of the conjectures made before his thorough investigation of Saxo's language and style.

Medieval fragments

Less than half a century after Stephanius' death the first fragment of a medieval codex of Saxo turned up (**C**). Apparently, it burned in 1728, but a collation of it survives (**c**). During the 19th century, more fragments of Saxo manuscripts were discovered in various Danish archives: **B, D** (probably parts of the same codex)[11] and **E**. These fragments from the last half of the 13th century showed that there was no reason to be seriously worried about the loss of complete medieval manuscripts of Saxo, because the fragments offered only few and rather insignificant new readings. It was concluded that **a** quite faithfully reproduces a medieval vulgate derived from one common ancestor, the archetype (**X**); careful analysis of quotations from Saxo by medieval authors and by Renaissance authors not using **a** (**F, K, O**) seemed also to corroborate this general view of the transmission of the text[12].

Such was the situation a hundred years ago, when the most recently discovered fragment, the so-called Angers fragment (**A**) came to light (1863), was identified (1877), and published (1879). The editor, Christian Bruun, explicitly warned scholars not to lose faith in **a**[13] because of the appearance of what seemed to be Saxo's autograph of Gesta Danorum, but serious doubts about the authenticity of **X** were soon raised by German and Danish scholars, culminating in 1927 with Hans Brix's philological investigation of **A**[14] and his conclusion that **X** was the product of a medieval editor superficially and mechanically reworking Saxo's draft (**A**) and making a smooth text out of it.

A renewal of the discussion of the authorship of the archetype (**X**) presupposes that three other problems in connection with **A** have been solved: Who wrote **A**? How big was the codex of which **A** is a fragment? What is the relationship between **A** and **X**?

(1) Bruun suggested that only some of the many interlinear supplements and variants in **A** were written by the same hand as the main text. This argument led scholars astray for some years, until it was convincingly demonstrated that the whole of the text of the fragment (except the marginal notes by the so-called "third" hand) is written by one and the same person, and that in all probability this person was Saxo himself, **A** being Saxo's own draft manuscript.

(2) A few years earlier, in 1920, Emil Rathsach[15] argued that the 14th century epitome of Saxo (**j**) was made directly from the Angers codex, the »third« hand being the author of the Compendium Saxonis preparing the text before epitomizing it, and it was concluded that the Angers codex contained *all* of Gesta Danorum. Not all of Rathsach's evidence is equally convincing, but his theory has gained general approval, and I shall, therefore, take it for granted that **A** is a fragment of Saxo's autographic draft of the whole of his work, not all that different in size and style from the version in **X**.

(3) As for the relation of **A** to **X**, there is general consensus that in spite of the substantial differences between the text of **A** and the corresponding part of **a**, **X** obviously descends from **A** in its "final" form, i.e. the main text with all the interlinear and marginal supplements and variants by the "first" and "second" hands (Saxo himself at three different stages of his work with the text).

A medieval editor?

There is no external evidence of a medieval editor of an unfinished draft of Gesta Danorum, and scholars quoting or interpreting Saxo as a rule tacitly imply that there is no real textual problem, i.e. that **X** was made by Saxo. However, the prevailing opinion in this century concerning the textual problems and the transmission of Saxo is that **X**, as suggested by Brix, was a careless version of the text offered by **A**, and that it contained such fatal misunderstandings of Saxo's intentions, that it could not possibly have been made by him.

A vigorous attempt to defend the authenticity of **X**, by Sofus Larsen, appeared in 1925[16]. Sofus Larsen showed that the version of the text in **a** is stylistically just as good as – if not better than – the version in **A**. This part of Sofus Larsen's long and learned investigation has never been challenged or surpassed, but unfortunately it was associated with a far-fetched and demonstrably incorrect answer he gave to another problem of some importance.

This problem concerns the source of **a**'s text, and the way in which Christiern Pedersen did his editorial work. In a short appendix to the paper mentioned above, Emil Rathsach had argued that there was evidence linking some of the elements ascribed by Bruun to the "third" hand with **X**, since a number of section marks in the margin of **A** are also found in **a** (and **K**). These section marks were assigned by Bruun to the 14th century (**j**, or contemporary with **j**), but now the 13th century vulgate, close to if not identical with **X**, became the terminus ante quem for the section marks in **A**. And if **X** contained elements derived from annotations in **A** that were not made by Saxo, Saxo's authorship of **X** could simply be ruled out.

This argumentation rests on two assumptions: (1) the section marks in **A** are so meaningless that they could not have been written by Saxo himself (and repeated by him in **X**); (2) the two sets of section marks in **A** and **a** are so similar that the section marks in **a** must derive from **A**. Both assumptions may be questioned, I believe, but Sofus Larsen found Rathsach's evidence conclusive, and in order to save **X**'s authenticity, he was compelled to link **A** with **a** in two different ways: through **X**, *and* through Christiern Pedersen.

Sofus Larsen suggested (1) that what Christiern Pedersen said in the letter mentioned above was that he originally had in his possession a manuscript of Saxo, but wanted to compare it with the old, damaged Angers codex he had heard about, and at last succeeded in getting hold of it; (2) that Christiern Pedersen contaminated the text of his first manuscript with readings, e.g. section marks[17], from the Angers codex.

Sofus Larsen's theory replaces a medieval editor of an unfinished Gesta Danorum with a Renaissance editor interpolating bits of "Ur-Saxo" (and later additions) into a finished Gesta Danorum. Of course, Sofus Larsen had to suggest that the codex used by Albert Krantz (**k**) at some stage had likewise been collated with and contaminated by the Angers codex, and his theory was immediately discarded by most Saxo scholars[19]. Sofus Larsen's polemical reply prompted a detailed analysis of the book-binding of which **A** had been a part, which proved beyond possible doubt that the Angers codex was cut to pieces and "lost" long before Christiern Pedersen was born[20].

This spectacular defeat meant that Sofus Larsen's theory of the transmission of the text, *and* his advocacy of the authenticity of **X** on stylistic grounds were considered to be definitely disproved. So, in the latest edition of Saxo, by Jørgen Olrik and Hans Ræder, it is stated in the Introduction that "the Angers fragment seems to demonstrate that Saxo did not have the opportunity to give the whole of his work the final touch". In itself, this does not sound very alarming, but it does imply that when we interpret Saxo's text, as historians or as philologists, we have to take into account not only the editorial work of Christiern Pedersen and his printer, and the possibility of errors creeping into the tradition from **X** to **g,** but we must also reckon with a medieval editor manipulating a draft that looked, in some parts at least, like the very chaotic Angers fragment. Such a model of the transmission explains, too, why Jørgen Olrik and Hans Ræder made so many conjectures and transpositions in their edition of 1931, based on the unfinished work of the German scholar C. Knabe. The editors were severely criticized for making conjectures whenever they thought Saxo could have expressed himself better than **a** does, but the basis of the editorial policy of Olrik and Ræder, i.e. their opinion of the archetype of **a,** was not seriously challenged until recently, when Jørgen Raasted reopened the debate by stating that Sofus Larsen's stylistic arguments in favour of the authenticity of **X** had been underestimated by Hans Brix, Olrik-Ræder, and many others. Jørgen Raasted did not, however, suggest any solution to the paradox of the section marks, which Sofus Larsen had not been able to solve.

After this sketch of some aspects of the transmission of Saxo's work, I shall try to add more evidence to that already collected by Sofus Larsen and Jørgen Raasted in favour of Saxo's authorship of **X**.

My evidence rests on a comparison of some rather formal aspects of the text given by **A** and **a,** such as prose rhythm, linguistic peculiarities, and technique of composition. However, since evidence of this kind will carry no conviction as long as other evidence seems to contradict it, I shall also discuss the problem raised by the section marks and suggest an explanation that is compatible with Saxo's authorship of **X**.

Prose rhythm

It has been an established fact for some forty years that there is plenty of *cursus* in our Gesta Danorum[22]. As long as no comprehensive, statistical study of the prose rhythm in the transmitted text has been made, no definite conclusions concerning the authenticity of **X** can possibly be drawn from analysis of the cursus appearing in the few prose pages of **A** and the corresponding part of **a**. But for the question at issue here, i.e. whether there is any evidence that an unfinished draft of Saxo's work (**A**) was carelessly edited by another than Saxo in the early 13th century, it may, after all, be worthwhile to take a closer look at the following four passages:

Ex. 1 (GD 12,13)

A, main text:	*tributi lége coércuit*	tardus
A, variant 1:	*tribúto adégit*	planus
A, variant 2:	*tributaria pensióne perdómuit*	tardus
a:	*tributaria ditióne perdómuit*	tardus

Ex. 2 (GD 12,18)

A, main text:	*ad summum gloriæ cumulum perduxit*	÷
A, variant:	*ad summum laudis cumulum perduxit*	÷
a:	*ad summum gloriæ státum prouéxit*	planus

Cf. GD 4,8: *ad laudis cúmulum perduxísti* (velox), and the following idioms in Valerius Maximus: *ad summum gloriæ cumulum peruenturi* (VM 3,1); *ad cumulum laudis perducitur* (VM 8,7).

Ex. 3 (GD 13,2)

A, main text:	*uires attinet*	÷
A, variant:	*uires attinebat*	÷
a:	*uíres attínuit*	tardus

Ex. 4 (GD 16,24)

A, main text:	*silentiique ulterióris impátiens*	tardus
A, variant:	*silentiique impatiens diuturnioris*	÷
a:	*silentiique diuturnióris impátiens*	tardus

As is the case with the imitation of Valerius Maximus and other classical authors (as demonstrated by Sofus Larsen and Jørgen Raasted), so, from the viewpoint of cursus, **a**'s relation to **A** is very much like the relation of the different stages in **A** to one another, leaving no room for a careless editor. In ex. 2 and ex. 3, cursus only appears in **a,** while in ex. 1 all four variants have an equally good cursus (*ditio* is found elsewhere in Gesta Danorum, 21,31 and 337,25, but this proves nothing, of course); in ex. 4 cursus is made to appear in **a** simply by inverting the words in the interlinear variant in **A;** so, a number of **a**'s deviations from **A,** which have hitherto looked like idle play with synonymous idioms, make sense from the viewpoint of prose rhythm.

Furthermore, ex. 2 is a particularly good example of the problem faced from time to time by an author with high stylistic ideals. From Valerius Maximus the author seems to have borrowed the idioms *ad cumulum laudis perducere* and *ad summum gloriæ cumulum;* by changing the order of the words *cumulum* and *laudis,* one can get a cursus with the inflected form *perduxisti* in GD 4,8, but the third person singular needed in GD 12,18 does not fit with a cursus, and so Valerius Maximus is dropped and another idiom *(ad...statum prouehere)* containing a paroxytone synonym to the proparoxytone *cumulum* is found in **a.**

Of course, a medieval editor of Saxo's draft may have become aware of Saxo's concern for cursus, and one may even imagine that a dedicated editor may have endeavoured to take special care not to spoil the rhythms in Saxo's text, but I find it difficult to believe that such a pious and careful editor would make arbitrary and unwarranted changes in his author's text, e.g. replacing *pensione* with *ditione* (ex. 1). Such changes originate with the author himself, more critical towards the product of his mind than any editor would be.

Absalon's codex of Valerius Maximus

Beside some shorter passages, there is one long sentence in **a** that has no counterpart in **A:**

> Idem [Scioldus] perditam et enervam vitam agentes continentiamque luxu labefacere solitos ad capessendam virtutem rerum agitatione sedulus excitabat (GD 12,6-8)

This clause was by some scholars thought to be an interpolation, but Sofus Larsen pointed out that it contains a number of reminiscences from Valerius Maximus. The fact that the sentence ends with a cursus velox *(sédulus excitábat)* points in the same direction, but there is more evidence in favour of the authenticity of this sentence.

The correct classical form of the fourth word in the sentence is not *enervus, -a, -um,* but *enervis, -e.* The adjective *enervus* is found in late medieval and Renaissance texts, and its appearance here may of course be due to a misprint in **a,** since the correct form *enervis, -e,* is found eleven times in Gesta Danorum, but another explanation must also be envisaged, for *enervus, -a, -um,* is attested in the codex of Valerius Maximus, which there is good reason to believe Saxo had at his disposal. But I must make a little digression on other possible instances of codex-specific imitation in Saxo before I produce the evidence about *enervam vitam.*

In a note to GD 213,31 on Saxo's use of the adjective *onustus* in a "wrong" sense (= *molestus, onerosus*), Stephanius (Notæ uberiores, p. 166) mentions that Caspar Barth suggested to correct *civibus etiam onustus* to *civibus etiam onus suis,* but Stephanius points out that Saxo has several instances of this "wrong" use of the adjective, and that, as appears from Pighius' notes to Valerius Maximus (printed 1567), some manuscripts have *onustos sibi* instead of the vulgate's *onerosos sibi* at VM 9,2, ext. 6, among which "præcipue eo codice, quem Saxonem nostrum semper ad manum habuisse nullus dubito, descriptum manu Absalonis Archiepiscopi quondam Lundensis, qui hodieque in Bibliotheca Hafniensi asservatur, mihique in emendando Saxone maximo sane usui fuit". This codex was not copied by Absalon, as Stephanius thought, but given by him to the monastery at Sorø (this is the meaning of the words *Liber sancte Marie de Sora per manum domni Absalonis Lundensis Archiepiscopi,* written on the last page). The codex burned in the University Library in 1728, but Stephanius personally made a complete collation of it in 1635, and this collation is now in the University Library in Uppsala, MS R 370[23]. Stephanius related this codex with Saxo, because it is stated in Absalon's will[24] that Saxo shall give the two manuscripts he has borrowed from him to monastery at Sorø[25].

Absalon's codex seems to have been a very close descendant of the "codex optimus" of Valerius Maximus, the famous Bernensis 366 from the 9th century, written for and corrected by Lupus of Ferrière before 860[26]: it has the lacuna in VM 1,1,4 that distinguishes the Bernensis from all other manuscripts known to the editor of the standard critical edition of Valerius Maximus[27]. An unabbreviated Valerius Maximus of such high quality must have been a rarity in the 12th century, and this sheds some light on the collaboration of Saxo and Absalon.

Stephanius's argumentation against Barth's conjecture GD 213,31 is brilliant and shows deep knowledge of Saxo's habits, but we may push his argument a little further. According to the Thesaurus linguae latinae, the corrupt passage of Valerius Maximus in question here, as given by the Bernensis, is the only instance recorded in classical authors of *onustus* (= *molestus* + the dative); Stephanius could not know that he had found the very passage in classical literature lying behind Saxo's repeated use of a "wrong" idiom, but his discovery is a very good example of Saxo's enthusiasm for out-of-the-way expressions warranted by his preferred stylistic model.

Other passages corroborate Stephanius' clever manuscript identification. Apparently without knowledge of the textual tradition of Absalon's codex of Valerius Maximus, Franz Blatt[28] has defended **a**'s *potientes* GD 62,4 against Jørgen Olrik's conjecture by referring to the Codex Bernensis, VM 3,2,20. And if we go back to the form *enervus, -a, -um*, which was the point of departure of this long digression, the Thesaurus linguae latinae informs us that one of the very few instances recorded of this form is, once again, our "Leit-codex" of Valerius Maximus, the Bernensis 366, VM 2,5,15 *enervos animos*. In the printed edition used for his collation of Absalon's codex, Stephanius has corrected the vulgate's *enerves animos* to *enervos animos*, as was to be expected. In this way, a closer look at *enervam vitam* can be made to testify to Saxo's authorship of the sentence found in **a**, but missing in **A**.

However, an explanation compatible with the theory of a medieval editor has been suggested by adherents of Brix's theory of the transmission: the sentence was originally in **A,** written beneath the long marginal supplement on the first folium of the fragment, some of which was later cut off when the Angers codex was destroyed and used for book-binding. This explanation would be quite convincing, if the sentence in question was printed in **a** at the place where one would expect to find it according to the theory, i.e. right after the long marginal supplement, but this is not the case, since it is to be found much earlier in the description of King Scioldus[29]. I think a solution to the problem may be found by analyzing the whole passage on King Scioldus on the assumption that Saxo is the author of both **A** and **X**.

The development of King Scioldus (GD 11,7-12,16)
A's main text (from GD 11,19, with interlinear variants) depicts a young, heroic, and conquering King Scioldus. The long marginal supplement

adds a new dimension to the young king's personality: he was not only a conqueror, but also a reformer, and a good, moral king. This aspect of Scioldus' personality is very loosely attached to his character as revealed in the main text, and if it is inserted where it is indicated in **A** that it should be, it spoils the train of thought, since the words *In quo annorum virtutisque procursu* ... are separated from the preceding sentence describing Scioldus' precocious virtues.

I suggest that when he reworked the whole passage, preparing **X**, Saxo realized that the supplement did not fit very well in the place where he had indicated earlier, in a preliminary way, that it should be inserted. Therefore, he moved the description of Scioldus' patriotism and reforms to where it stands in **a**, i.e. just before the mention of his marriage to Alvilda and the description of his son Gram. (The omission of Alvilda's high social rank, *Saxonum regis puellam* according to **A**, may also be due to Saxo, since it makes Scioldus all the more important, and his relation to Alvilda more elevated). At the same time, Saxo inverted the sequence of some of the sentences within the long marginal supplement, thus making it somewhat more logical than in its preliminary form; he also added a further reflection on what he had written earlier in the marginal supplement: *Acrem poenam exegit, tamquam in omnium libertorum poenam unius crimen redundare par esset,* a sentence that is generally considered to be an interpolation because it is not found in **A**.

But Saxo may still have had a feeling that his King Scioldus consisted of two loosely combined parts, and therefore, I suggest, he added the sentence *Idem...excitabat* earlier in the description of Scioldus, thus pointing out that already in his youth he displayed the *patriæ caritas* to be described at length a little later.

Section marks in **A** *and* **a**

As mentioned earlier, a number of section marks in **A**, all considered to be post-Saxonian, but apparently repeated in **X**, since they are also found in **a** (and **K**), have been taken as evidence against Saxo's authorship of **X**. The section marks appear in the margin of the versified dialogue of Gro and Besse, GD 14,1-16,22.

The Gro-Besse dialogue is a very sophisticated piece of literary composition: Gro and Besse each make 5 statements, amounting to a total of exactly 100 lines (2 distichs, 87 adoneans, and 9 short prose lines)[30]; as they appear in **A**, the 96 short lines of mixed prose and verse look like

one long, uninterrupted row of verse lines (all end with a full stop, but
Saxo has taken great care that none of the prose lines scan as an adone-
an); the 15-lined pages of **A** fit astonishingly well into the structure of the
100 lines, so that the two columns of adoneans start on the top of a new
page (the 15-lined pages also fit perfectly into the following Gro-Gram
dialogue, one page further than the Angers fragment, until GD 17,19);
the number 96 is very flexible and allows for various forms of lay-out:
6x16, 4x24 (so **a!** – modern editions spoil Saxo's consistently artistic lay-
out), 3x32, 2x48.

The contents of the dialogue are rather difficult to grasp, but the
situation seems to be that Bessus acts as match-maker between his friend
Gram and Gro, a Swedish princess, but Gro rejects the proposal. Some
obscure points in the dialogue indicate that Saxo translated a poem he
did not fully understand, but as a piece of Latin artistry it is a master-
piece: dense, dramatic phrasing coupled with humour and glimpses of
truly human reactions.

There is some confusion about the number of section marks in **A**:
Bruun has 5, Rathsach mentions only 4 (misprint?), and Sofus Larsen
counts 6 out of the 10 possible positions:

		Bruun	Rathsach	Larsen
Pos. 1	Gro: *Conspicor ...*	x	x	x
	2 distichs			
Pos. 2	*Tum Bessus sic orsus*			
	7 adoneans			
Pos. 3	*Ad hæc Gro*			
	7 adoneans			
Pos. 4	*Cui Bessus*			
	7 adoneans			
Pos. 5	*Tum Gro*			
	8 adoneans			
Pos. 6	*Contra sic Bessus*	x	x	x
	11 adoneans			
Pos. 7	*Rursum Gro*	x	x	x
	14 adoneans			
Pos. 8	*Item Bessus*	x	x	x
	13 adoneans			
Pos. 9	*Ad quem Gro*			x
	9 adoneans			
Pos. 10	*Ad quam Bessus*	x		x
	11 adoneans			

Saxonis Grammatici

adesse rata:simulq̃ tam insoliti cult⁹ horrore muliebriter territa:succussis frenis ma-
xima cum totius corporis trepidatione patrio carmine sic cœpit.
Conspicor inuisum regi venisse gigantem
   Et gressu medias obtenebrare vias:
Aut oculis fallor:nam tegmine sæpe ferino
   Contigit audaces delituisse viros.

Cui Bess⁹ sic orf⁹.
Virgo caballi
Quę premis armos
Verba vicissim
Mutua fundens
Quod tibi nomen
Qua fueris dic
Gente creata!
   Ad hæc Gro.
Gro mihi nomen:
Rex pater extat
Sanguine fulgens
Fulgidus armis.
Tu quoqʒ qui fis
Aut satus vnde
Promito nobis.
   Cui Bessus.
Bessus ego sum
Fortis in armis
Trux inimicis
Gentibus horror
Atqʒ alieno
Sæpe refundens
Ságuine dextram.

Tum Gro.
Quis rogo vestrũ
Dirigit agmen!
Quo duce signa
Bellica fertis!
Quis moderatur
Prælia princeps
Quove paratur
Præstite bellum!
CCôtra sic Bessus.
Gram regit agmē
Marte beatus:
Quē met⁹ aut vis
Flectere nescit
Nec rogus ardens
Nec ferus ensis
Aut maris vnḡ
Terruit æstus.
Hoc duce belli
Signa leuamus
Aurea virgo.
CRursum Gro.
Hinc remeantes
Vertite cursum

Ne proprio vos
Opprimat omnes
Agmine Sictrug:
Inqʒ feroci
Stipite figat
Illaqueato
Guttura nexu
Detqʒ rigenti
Corpora nodo
Ac male totuus
Trudat edaci
Funera coruo.
C Iterum Bessus.
Gram prior illum
Manibus addet
Ac dabit orcho:
Qʒ sua fatis
Lumina claudat
Inqʒ pauenda
Vertice plexum
Tartara mittet.
Nulla Sueuorum
Castra timemus
Quid minitaris

Tristia nobis
Funera virgo!
CAd quem Gro.
En ferar istinc
Nota reuisens
Tecta parentis
Ne venientis
Conspicer audax
Agmina fratris.
Vos remeantes
Vltima queso
Fata morentur.
CAd quam Bessus
Leta reuise
Nata parentem
Nec cita nobis
Fata precare:
Nec tua bilis
Pectora pulset.
Namqʒ petenti
Aspera primum
Difficilisqʒ
Sepe secundo
Fœmina cedit.

Post hæc Gram horrendæ monstruosęqʒ vocis habitum trucioris soni modulis ęmu-
latus,silentiisqʒ diuturnioris impatiens,talibus puellam dictis aggreditur.
Ne timeat rabidi germanum virgo gigantis:
   Me neqʒ contiguum palleat esse sibi.
A Grip missus enim nunḡ nisi compare voto
   Fulcra puellarum concubitumqʒ peto.
         Cui Gro.
Quæ sensus exors scortum velit esse gigantum
   Aut quæ monstriferum possit amare thorum!
Quæ coniunx fore dæmonum Possit monstrigeni conscia seminis!
Suumqʒ gigantifero consociare velit cubile!
Quis spina digitos fouet!Quis syncęra luto misceat oscula!
Quis membra iungat hispida lęuibus impariter locatis!
Cum natura reclamitat:haud plenum Veneris carpitur otium:
Nec congruit monstris amor fœmineo celebratus vsu.

Fig 1: Paris editon, 1514, fol. IV verso (= GD 13,7–17,10)

This confusion is due to the fact that the section marks are not all alike. Sofus Larsen's at pos. 9 may not be a section mark at all, but is an abbreviation of the word *Contra* written by the "third" hand (Bruun). While the "third" hand's notes at pos. 1 and pos. 6 are posterior to the section mark, the section mark at pos. 8 must have been written after (or at the same time as) the marginal note, since it stands below the line it refers to; it also differs very much in size and shape from the remaining section marks, except pos. 9, and I therefore suggest that pos. 8 and pos. 9 belong to the "third" hand, while the section marks at pos. 1, 6, 7, and 10, belong to an older series of section marks. Having encountered the two section marks at pos. 6 and pos. 7, the "third" hand mechanically added them at pos. 8 and pos. 9, too.

If we now turn to **a,** we find a quite different pattern. Every shift in the dialogue is marked typographically, either with a blank space (pos. 1 – pos. 5), or by a section mark (pos. 6 – pos. 10). One may well ask whether this system of blanks and section marks needs to be derived from the section marks in **A** (**a**'s system fits well with a lay-out with 3 columns on one page (3x22): blanks in the left margin, section marks in the two inner margins), but in view of the fact that the section marks found elsewhere in **a** are also found in **K** (in another poetical dialogue, GD 224,28-228,16), as pointed out by Rathsach, it is better not to reject the evidence of the section marks as fortuitous. Of course, one may argue that if Saxo did write **X**, he would probably repeat the beautiful but confusing lay-out of the Gro-Besse dialogue in **A,** prompting any reader or copyist of a common ancestor to **a** and **k** to indicate in some way or other every time there is a change of speaker (= every prose line). This may be the correct solution to the problem, but I shall suggest another one which I find preferable, since it accounts for the "old" series of section marks in **A.**

The section marks in **A** (5 or 6 in number) have always been interpreted as intending to express the same as the blanks and section marks in **a,** but there has been no explanation of why this aim was not reached. However, if we isolate a set of four "old" section marks, this set makes sense as a formal and semantic segmentation of the 100 lines of the Gro-Besse dialogue into four blocks of 37, 12, 39, and 12 lines. On the semantic level, the blocks contain:

1) Presentation of Gro and Bessus
2) Presentation of Gram (marriage proposal)

3) Gro's refusal

4) A renewed proposal.

Although this looks very elementary, I think no one but Saxo himself could have been aware of the structure underlying this bewildering dialogue. When reviewing his text, he changed very little in the poetical parts, but he may have found it necessary to give some assistance to the reader by pointing out the main segments of the text – without, however, spoiling the effect of the 96 visually identical and continuous lines. In the transmission of the text, Saxo's section marks, repeated by him in **X**, were misunderstood as (incomplete) indications of a new speaker, and this resulted in the typographical devices we find in **a**, and in the two supplementary section marks added by the "third" hand in **A**.

The discovery of the Angers fragment has contributed very much to our understanding of Saxo' style, his method of composition, etc. But even after more than a hundred years of research, this fascinating piece of parchment may yield new insights into Saxo's very complex mind. And if we reject the exaggerated »Echtheitskritik« of the 19th century and accept Saxo as the author of **X**, we can also watch Saxo in the next stage of his endeavour to give his Gesta Danorum the most accomplished and sophisticated form.

NOTES

[1] *Tre latinske grammatikker.* Ed. Erik Dal & Jan Pinborg, København 1979, p. 176.

[2] A small number of the misprints were corrected in the course of the printing and are only found in some of the copies. Cf. SAXONIS GRAMMATICI *Historia Danica.* Rec. P.E. Müller & J.M. Velschow, vol. 1, Copenhagen 1839, p. XI, n. 1; LAURITZ NIELSEN, *Dansk Bibliografi 1482-1550,* København 1919, p. 113.

[3] C.F. WEGENER, *Historiske Efterretninger om Anders Sørensen Vedel,* København 1851, p. 79, n. 1.

[4] Many of Vedel's corrections are falsely attributed to Stephanius in all editions, e.g. GD 23,21 »Lemmer« Vedel (= *artus* Stephanius): *arcus* **a**; GD 279,19 »Clenodie oc Eiendom« Vedel (= *censui* Stephanius): *sensui* **a**.

[5] J.E. SANDYS, *A history of classical scholarship,* vol. 2, Cambridge 1908, p. 364.

[6] E.g. *Notæ uberiores,* p. 37C (ad GD 18,2) where Stephanius says that Barth's advocacy of the reading of his manuscript »e diametro pugnare videtur cum ipsis Saxonis verbis«.

[7] His *Breves notæ ac emendationes in nobilissimum rerum Danicarum scriptorem Saxonem Grammaticum* were published in Leiden 1627.

[8] H.D. Schepelern in the introduction (p. 12) to the facsimile edition of the *Notæ uberiores* (Danish Humanist Texts and Studies, 2), Copenhagen 1978; cf. also JØRGEN RAASTED, 'Frants Nielsen fra Grenå og Stephanius' Saxonoter', *Museum Tusculanum* vol. 34-35 (1979) p. 80ff.

[9] Karsten Christensen, *Om overleveringen af Sven Aggesens værker*, København 1978 (Skrifter udgivet af Det historiske Institut ved Københavns Universitet, 10), p. 68 ff.

[10] Povl Johs. Jensen, 'Madvig som filolog', in *Johan Nicolai Madvig. Et mindeskrift*, vol. 2, København 1963, p. 90 ff.

[11] Erik Kroman, *Saxo og Overleveringen af hans Værk*, København 1971 (Studier fra Sprog- og Oldtidsforskning, 278), p. 72, denies that this was the codex used by Christiern Pedersen for printing **a**, as suggested by Ellen Jørgensen, 'Chr. Pedersens Saxocodex', in Victor Madsen, *Et Saxoproblem*, København 1930, p. 39.

[12] Chr. Bruun, *Angers-Fragmentet af et Haandskrift af Saxo Grammaticus*, København 1879 (Lykønskningsskrift til Kjøbenhavns Universitets Firehundredaars Stiftelsesfest), p. XVIII.

[13] Id., ibid., p. XXV, n. 3.

[14] Hans Brix, 'Om Angersfragmentet af Saxo', *Aarbøger for nordisk Oldkyndighed og Historie* 1927, p. 191 ff.

[15] Emil Rathsach, 'Om den saakaldte 3. Haand i Angersfragmentet af Saxos Danmarkshistorie', *Aarbøger for nordisk Oldkyndighed og Historie* 1920, p. 112 ff.

[16] Sofus Larsen, 'Saxo Grammaticus, hans Værk og Person', *Aarbøger for nordisk Oldkyndighed og Historie* 1925, p. 1 ff.

[17] Concerning the much-debated problem of *Item/Iterum* at GD 15,25, cf. Erik Kroman's reasonable solution (op. cit., p. 71): at some stage between **A** and **a**, an abbreviated *Item* was misinterpreted as *Iterum*, independently of the note in **A** by the "third" hand.

[18] Thomas Riis, *Les institutions politiques centrales du Danemark 1100-1332*, Odense 1977 (Odense University Studies in History and Social Sciences, 46), p. 30, has tried to prove that Christiern Pedersen even tampered with the book-division in Gesta Danorum.

[19] Carl S. Petersen in the introduction to *Apoteker Sibbernsens Saxobog*, København 1927.

[20] Victor Madsen, *Et Saxoproblem. Angers-Fragmenterne og Christiern Pedersen*, København 1930.

[21] Jørgen Raasted, 'Angersfragmentet og Saxo-overleveringen', in *Saxostudier*. Red. Ivan Boserup, København 1975 (Opuscula Graecolatina, 2), p. 54 ff.

[22] Bertil Axelson, 'Satsrytm hos Saxo', *Scandia*, vol. 9 (1936) p. 204ff.

[23] A microfilm of Uppsala R 370 is in the Royal Library in Copenhagen, MS micro 1725.

[24] *Notæ uberiores*, p. 6D: »In Testamento Absalonis MS. quod in mea Bibliotheca asservatur ...«

[25] Absalon's will was first published in 1696; the other manuscript has been identified with a codex of Justinus in the Royal Library (Gl. kgl. Saml. 450 fol.), and this identification is corroborated by the fact that it has exactly the same »per manum« formula as the one reported by Stephanius from the codex of Valerius Maximus.

[27] C. Kempf in the Teubner Series, 1888 (1966^2), p. XXV.

[28] Franz Blatt in the Prolegomena (p. VI) to his Saxo lexicon, Copenhagen 1957.

[29] Olrik and Ræder have printed the sentence at GD 12,6, right after the text of the long marginal supplement, thus implying that the medieval editor displaced the sentence to the place where it is found in **a**.

[30] Jens Juhl Jensen, 'Bjarkemålet – latinsk lyrik eller dansk digtning?' *Museum Tusculanum*, vol. 27 (1976) p. 53f., has analyzed the numerological pattern in the 87 adoneans (3x29, etc.).

THE PLACE OF FICTION IN SAXO'S LATER BOOKS

ERIC CHRISTIANSEN

New College, University of Oxford

In Saxo's time, the word *fictio* still kept its old classical meanings. It could be used to describe any made object, including works of literature; thus Man was God's fiction, and all the works of man were fictional – or fictile. It could be used as a word of blame, for any form of literature that was not strictly true, like mythology, epic, or drama. Therefore, no-one appears to have sat down and decided to write a work of fiction as opposed to a work of fact. And, it was perfectly respectable to write works of fact in the form of fiction: Bernard Silvestris, Alan of Lille, and John of Hautville, among others, did so.

Historians writing in the twelfth century were often sensitive to the charge of falsification. Those who wrote about the distant past were apt to substantiate their stories by ascribing them to ancient authors, records and traditions. Those who wrote about modern times liked to justify themselves by referring to their own qualifications as eye-witnesses, or friends of eye-witnesses, or as collectors and sifters of current rumour. When they apologized for their imperfect literary skill, they implied that truth was better unvarnished; when they boasted of their Latinity, they asserted that truth was at least one of the beauties they had to offer. The biggest liar of them all, Geoffrey of Monmouth, pretended that he was the translator of an authoritative version of the History of Britain. Saxo also insisted that his own writings were 'non tam recenter conflata quam antiquitus edita'; he promised his readers 'non nugacem sermonis luculentiam, sed fidelem vetustatis notitiam'.

However, there can be little doubt that in his history of the pre-conversion Danes, contrivance is king. Despite his use of runic inscriptions, ancient traditions, and learned Icelanders, he makes what he wants out of what they told him. But in Books X to XIII, he used written sources and fixed traditions that contained a nucleus of what we might call history;

and in Books XIV to XVI he drew on the reminiscenses of Absalon and others whose memories stretched back to the 1140s, and perhaps on his own experience. This material ought not to have been so plastic; yet it had to be worked up to conform to the patterns and programmes which unify the whole work. The question therefore arises of what exactly were the processes which the raw material had to undergo before it became the finished product. On the answer to this depends the answer to another: how reliable a source was Saxo for the history of the twelfth century?

To begin with, it is obvious that in the later as in the earlier books, the material is more or less rhetoricized. This appears both in the set orations attributed to Canute Lavard, Domborus, Absalon, and in the continual use of what were originally tricks of the advocate's trade. The commonest examples are devices prescribed by Priscian in his Grammar: the narration, the anecdote, the *sententia,* the *topos,* the comparison, the impersonation or *ethopoeia,* the description, the *positio.* All are deployed according to the doctrines either of Priscian, or of Cicero, or of the *Auctor ad Herennium,* and all naturally involve pushing the material into shape. This was the consequence of a training in *dictamen,* and if it involved distortion, hardly deserves to be called fiction.

At the same time, it is possible to find instances of what looks like downright fabrication. In Book XII there is the story of how King Eric the Good went on pilgrimage to Constantinople, and died at Cyprus *en route* for Jerusalem. The outline of the story had been written in an early source, the *Historia Sancti Canuti* of Robert of Ely, now lost, but preserved in a 16th century epitome. It appears that Saxo had access to this work, and also perhaps to legends about Eric that could have been preserved at his birthplace of Slangerup; but whatever his data, it can hardly have dictated the bizarre form which the story of the pilgrimage takes in Book XII.

It is embellished with two anecdotes that had nothing to do with Eric. One concerned the ancient problem of the power of music, and told how a man had been driven mad by a particular mode. As early as the time of Quintilian, the ancients had been asking, what man? what mode? and what musician? and had come up with various answers. Saxo's answers were: Eric the Good of Denmark, the Phrygian mode, and a certain musician who arrived at the Danish court and boasted of his skill. He needed an explanation of how a virtuous but over-energetic ruler could have done something so criminal that it justified the most laborious of all expiations; this story provided it. When Eric got to Byzantium, it was clear that something remarkable had to happen. This was where Harold Hardrada and Sigurd Jorsalfari had distinguished themselves, and what a Norwegian king could do, a Danish king could do better. But the evidence was most unsatisfactory; even Markús Skeggjason's *Eiríksdrápa* said little about this momentous occasion. However, there was a story of how the Byzantine emperor sent spies to learn the intentions of the pilgrim Charlemagne; and there was a tradition that the Varangian guards were the most loyal troops in the Roman army, when sober. Put them together, and you have the tale of how Eric disarmed the suspicions of the Emperor's spy by haranguing the emigré Danish Varangians on the virtues of loyalty and sobriety.

In these two cases, there was a gap between what Saxo was told, and what he wanted to say, and he filled it in much the same way as he had filled other gaps in Denmark's prehistory. Perhaps he did this on later occasions as well, but it is impossible to prove because there is so little chance of catching him out: *caute confingendum est* was one of the precepts of the *Auctor ad Herennium* which he took to heart. When he made Cardinal Nicholas Breakspear dissuade King Sweyn of Denmark from attacking Sweden with the analogy of the spider's web and the insects, he was certainly fabulating, because the war must have been fought before the cardinal arrived; but at least he made Nicholas use the kind of parable which according to John of Salisbury, who knew Breakspear well, he was apt to use.

So, in the later books, Saxo often rhetoricizes, and sometimes fabulates. This hardly needs repeating. At the same time he claimed to be writing true history. This raises the question: true in what sense?

Let us note that he had access to very little of what would now be called authentic historical evidence, and that what made this material historical evidence in his eyes was simply that it was about the past – not that it satisfied strict criteria of reliability. It might appear that in the last three books there was little need for pure fabrication, because of the abundance of data. But written records and eye-witness accounts enjoy a special status in our scale of reliability which in Saxo's they lacked. The casual way he treated his only 'good' sources, Adam of Bremen and the Roskilde Chronicle, proves it. He seems to have ranked his sources like this:

(i) Absalon's reminiscenses – sacrosanct because of the rank and worth of Absalon.

(ii) Other word-of-mouth information; less reliable, but never discounted simply because oral.

(iii) Written history, frequently ignored, or dismissed as unreliable and partizan.

With this scale of values, there was no reason why sheer invention should not have played as important a part in Books XIII to XVI as in Books I to XII. On the other hand, it is not unreasonable to assume that word-of-mouth information about the events of the twelfth century was more reliable than traditions about the remoter past, and sometimes more reliable than the written sources to which Saxo applied. He is likely to have been accurate without meaning to be. Even so, the process of selection and presentation gave him scope for invention and perhaps for fiction.

This brings to me a topical question. How far did Saxo's underlying philosophical principles determine what he wrote? Kurt Johannesson has shown us how to deduce what these principles were; but the extent to which they are mirrored in the text of the later books deserves a closer look. Let us consider two examples from Book XIV.

It has been pointed out that Saxo's circumstantial account of the events of June to October 1157 contains some very dubious assertions. For example, the Lund Necrology establishes that the battle of Gråhede, which put an end to the reign of Sweyn III, was fought on October 23rd 1157, at a time of year which in Jutland could almost be called early winter. Yet Saxo claims that on that day the fields were still thick with standing corn, and that king Sweyn's horses had eaten so much of it that they were too bloated to charge when the moment came. He also claims that before the battle a dense flock of crows flew into King Valdemar's army so low that they could be struck down with lances – when we know that crows never fly low unless about to settle, and flocks of crows never settle in the proximity of living men. He also claims that Valdemar's army was so large that the King's own banner was only visible to one tenth of it – which would make the army extend about five miles in each direction. Insignificant details – innocent epic commonplaces – perhaps. It all depends on how we interpret the whole sequence from the murder of Canute V to the triumph of Valdemar.

It is possible to accept all the details and incidents in this sequence as representations of a conflict in which the macro-cosmic elements, and most of the micro-cosmic arts and sciences take sides with Valdemar against a Sweyn who has become as primally obnoxious to the created world as Rufinus, in the poem written against him by Claudian.

Thus: the earth gives way under his retreating feet, when he wanders into a bog and loses his retainers and his horses. Water continually keeps him away from the enemy he is pursuing, in the shape of the sea and the rivers at Randers. The fire which he has removed from the hall at Roskilde to aid his treachery, in fact leaves a darkness in which Valdemar escapes. The tempests of the air allow Valdemar's boat to sail from Zealand to Jutland unpursued. The liberal arts are enlisted on Valdemar's side in the rhetoric which wins him the support of the Jutlanders at the Viborg *ting* and loses Sweyn his fleet when he lands in Jutland; in the dialectic by which he deduces Sweyn's murderous intentions before the deed; in the comic branch of grammatical skill embodied in the witticisms of Absalon and Esbern, and in the dramatic as well, when disguise and subterfuge assist the royal escape. Music appears in the song of Valdemar's minstrel before battle. Of the mechanical arts, there are examples in the carpentry that puts a repaired boat at Valdemar's disposal, the navigation that steers it over the sea, the dyeing or painting that makes the tunics of his levies look like metal, the *ars militaris* that outwits Sweyn in battle, weaving in the cloak and girdle that foil his assassination plot and so on. Seen from this point of view, the standing corn will symbolize the art of husbandry, the crows that of augury, and the incredible numbers of the Valdemarine army will reflect the art of arithmetic.

But is this pattern really there? Whether it is or not, there are certainly other ways of interpreting the story. It could equally well be seen as a psychomachy, a battle between the virtues of the Valdemarines and the vices of Sweyn, in which the hand of God tips the scale in favour of the innocent. Or it could be seen as a forensic exercise, a detailed *narratio* to serve as an indictment, proving both the guilt of the accused *in re,* and the manifest consequences of that guilt *post rem.* And some may consider this narration to be primarily a study in nemesis, the concluding act of the tragedy of king Sweyn told in this way primarily for dramatic effect. Instead of pausing to discuss these possibilities, I hasten on to another example: the account of the conquest of the Rugians and the fall of Arkona.

These events were seen at the time as a triumph of Christ and his followers over the Devil, and Saxo evidently shared this view. He describes the idols of the Rugians and their cults, mentions the visible demon that left the shrine of Svantovitus when it was destroyed, and by his own allusions to providence and the faith leaves no doubt in his readers' minds that these were *Gesta Dei per Danos*. He even has a miracle story at the end.

But there is another pattern also, visible in the dominant part played by natural forces in the siege of Arkona. An accidental collapse of the earthworks defending the gateway of the fortress reveals an approach to the timber defences. A childish game between the boys on either side brings this approach to the notice of an anonymous Danish youth. He lights a fire below the walls with some straw (which happened to be carted by at the time) and the wind happened to fan the fire into a blaze that destroyed the gate-tower and threatened to overwhelm the entire fortress. To emphasize the amazing good luck that this amounted to, we are told that the elaborate siege-preparations ordered by the King and Absalon were unnecessary; the timber machines had to be dismantled later, and used to build a church. And when the Rugians tried to quench the flames with milk, they only blazed the fiercer. Here, if you like, were the four elements fighting for Denmark, and in this case the identity of the Danish cause with the will of the Creator made it an appropriate fiction.

At this point, the reader would deduce that Arkona was doomed. But Saxo points out that it wasn't – not yet, anyway. The fire would have died down. The walls could have been rebuilt. The garrison could have regained heart and fought on – their courage and desperation were not in doubt. The Danes could have quarrelled among themselves, as so often they did. And even if they had stormed the fortress in the end, the sack of Arkona would have deterred other Rugian warriors from submitting to the Danes. They could have won the fort and lost the war.

Of course, all this was not to be, because the penetrating intelligence of Bishop Absalon summed up the situation, and acting on his advice, the King and Archbishop Eskil used their authority and rhetoric to bring about a conditional surrender and a conversion of the whole garrison. Psychology, dialectic and political science are the branches of reason which put a bridle on fortune, and create victory from the makings of victory.

There seems to be no easy way of discovering how much violence was done to the facts, or the evidence, by this method of writing. Too often, Saxo is the only source. It is arguable that by making up his mind about how and why things happened, he made it difficult to say exactly what happened. The formulae he accepted as his starting point were not based on historical evidence, therefore the historical evidence he used to prove them was liable to be doctored. This was a common practise among mediaeval historians, but none of them is quite like Saxo. They share his belief in the hand of God as a historical force, his political partisanship, and some of his psychological assumptions, but they lack his pervading Platonism, just as he lacks the framework of annalistic records and historiographical tradition in which they wrote.

I mentioned Platonism, and by this I understand a scientific explanation of the universe derived from the Timaeus by way of Chalcidius, and then perhaps William of Conches, and a number of other possible interpreters. In this explanation, the appearance of things is seen as the accidental form taken by underlying realities. The highest duty of man is to perceive the reality behind the form and thus come closer to understanding the mind of the Creator. Therefore the concept of the visible happening is not all-important; it is merely the starting point for a train of reasoning that ought to lead back to the source of being.

The contrast between appearance and reality is evident throughout the work. For example, in the account of the conspiracy of the Danish princes against Canute Lavard, Saxo carefully traces the victory of the passions and the vices in the minds of the conspirators that determined the action they took, and were merely cloaked by what they professed beforehand. He may have had some evidence about what actually happened when Canute was assassinated, but he cannot have had any about what the assassins were thinking; yet he relates both with equal confidence, and implies that the passions were the reality, the gestures the form. The doomed prince was given a last warning by the minstrel who sang him the story of the treachery of Grimhild and her brothers – a fiction that ought to have revealed the facts. This, and the other conspiracies of 1167 and 1176 naturally lent themselves to the detection of realities lying behind appearances. It would seem that to Saxo all situations offered the same scope; as when he presented the varied relationship between Absalon and Valdemar as a set of exemplars determined by the *conglutinatio animarum* which Cicero had portrayed as the highest form of friendship.

Nothing is allowed to exist of itself; everything illustrates or denotes something else. Some of Saxo's favourite words are *exemplum, experimentum, documentum, species, specimen, similitudo, involucrum, figmentum* – continually intruded to remind the reader that the forms things take are not the whole story. But what is the whole story?

Whatever may lie in the background of his narrative, the foreground is occupied by life-like portrayals of incident. This appears to come from eye-witness reports. So they may have, in Books XIV to XVI: but since they occur in all books, and since most books are confections of ancient legend, the authenticity of the later examples must be open to doubt.

The purpose of these brief 'scenes' becomes easier to understand by looking again at the purpose of the whole work. In the preface, and elsewhere, Saxo explains that he was engaged in a battle against oblivion. Time, and illiteracy, had obscured the Danish past, and he intended to rescue it. He was restoring the national memory, ostensibly by interpreting the rude monuments and unpolished traditions of his ancestors, in fact by stocking it with a mass of historical events derived from a variety of likely and unlikely sources. As a trained classicist he knew that there was a whole science devoted to remembrance: the study known as *Memoria,* or Mnemotechnics, which Frances Yates herself rescued from oblivion a few years ago. He would not have known of any fully developed mnemonic scheme, since the authors of the twelfth century appear to have worked out individual mnemonic devices rather than employing one or two master-plans. Nevertheless, the principles of Memoria were adequately stated in the *Ad Herennium,* and echoed in many other works, and amounted to this: Arguments and events could be kept in mind by associating them with places and things that had an immediate visual impact. For, wrote the *Auctor ad Herennium,* 'it is just as easy to remember things in the form of carefully emphasized fictions, as it is to remember them when they are true'. Note the assumption that the same thing can be both real and fictional, at least, for the purpose of argument.

The story of the English scribe who reinvigorated a demoralized Danish raiding-party by recalling the past glories of the nation indicates how Saxo hoped his work would be put to practical use. But how would it be remembered? It had only the barest chronological framework, and the weight of commentary and implication attached to each story interrupted and sometimes spoiled the narration. Something more was needed to prevent the reader becoming confused and over-taxed.

The answer was provided by poetry, geography, and symbolic imagery. The poems of the earlier books, with their surprisingly diverse metres, were, among other things, examples of the oldest mnemonic art of all; their effect was expressed in the phrase *ut pictura poesis*. In the later books, memory is helped by devices suitable to prose, and among these I would class both location, and the combination of anecdote and image.

For examples, consider the many striking and symbolic incidents that punctuate his description of the wars against the Slavs. These remain in my mind much more clearly than other parts of the narrative, and I suspect they were meant to. The exhausted crews sleeping under their ship-awnings and woken by Eskil with a joke about the dead under their mounds; the Slav who drowns himself from fear of death, the Slav who hangs himself from fear of capture; the Danish captain so confident that he beaches on an enemy coast to repair his ship; Absalon's spy waving his hat from a cliff-top; the walls of Szczecin bristling with Danish arrows; swallows nesting in the prows of Danish ships for want of shelter on the devastated Slav mainland; Bogyslaus drinking before battle, Bogyslaus falling off his horse, Bogyslaus dead drunk under the protection of Absalon's retainers – these are all things that probably happened, but they are still *res fictae* because they symbolize rather than state the truth.

In other words, the fiction consists not of the story itself, but of the way it is told, and its relation to the narrative. The story is not there just because it happened, but because among the many things that happened it seemed to stand out as symbolic. In this, the anecdote, the oration, the *sententia,* and the description are alike; different devices for expressing the same truths.

This method enabled Saxo to select a wide variety of reported happenings and present them as more or less equivalent manifestations of the truth. For example, in dealing with the Scanian revolts against Absalon and his followers, he offers at least four kinds of phenomena which are usually regarded as distinct. First, there are the premonitory signs and auguries – the mass-drowning of the singing mice in Schleswig fjord, and the gnawing of Absalon's clothes as he slept. Then there is the interplay of passion among the rebels, the Scanian clergy, the Scanian nobility, and the supporters of Absalon – a conflict in which the frailty of the human mind is brought out more clearly than any specific grievances that might have caused the movement. Thirdly, there are the battles and assemblies which made up the chronicle of the revolt. Fourthly there is the diagnosis, treatment, and resolution of the affair that came from Absalon himself. These categories are intermingled at every stage, but there is no attempt to determine which were the most significant. There was no need for this, because anyone who had read the previous books of Saxo's history would be well aware that this particular tumult was merely a manifestation of certain underlying truths: that Scanians were rebellious and obstinate, that mobs were fickle and hysterical, that plebeians were unfit to exercise power, that discipline won battles, that Jutlanders were unreliable, and that Absalon had mastered the science of politics.

Earlier on, I asked the question: how far did Saxo's underlying philosophical principles determine what he wrote? It has not yet been answered. But since Dr. Johannesson is present at this symposium, it must not be overlooked. He has made this the most interesting of Saxo-problems, and it bears directly on the matter of fiction.

Perhaps it can best be approached by asking another question. How far are the contents of the work determined by geography? It begins with a geographical survey, and indications and sometimes descriptions of places occur in all the books. It evidently mattered greatly to the author that his readers should know not only where, but in what sort of places things had happened. Yet it would be absurd to deduce that this mattered more than anything else; it was not the places themselves that were important, but what happened at them. They are map references that fix events in the reader's mind by linking them with a geographical framework: as the author puts it 'I shall relate all things ... more vividly (speciosius) if the course of this history first traverse the places to which the events belong'.

By analogy, the philosophical framework, within which these events are also fixed, can be seen as a system of reference. By a framework, I understand precisely such a table of virtues, arts, and rhetorical modes as Dr. Johannesson has reconstructed in his book: a map of the mental world which the educated reader would have firmly imprinted on his mind. The map itself is not what is being expounded in the history; its function is to make the history more memorable, in the same way as the geographical references. In the earlier books, the influence of the system appears greater, because the contents are evidently more artificial and malleable; in the last three, Absalon's reminiscenses provide so much more complex and detailed a narrative that the possible references outgrow the earlier framework. In the two examples I chose from Book XIV, the search for archetypes and symbols and interpretations did not lead back to any one master plan. On the contrary, the fall of Sweyn III and of Arkona appear to be described in a way that creates intellectual waves receding in different directions to the horizon of the mental world. There is political propaganda, the miraculous, the liberal arts, psychological theory, rhetoric, psychomachy, and so on; but these are echoes, rather than explanations or determinants of what happened. To classify them as aids to memory rather than as anything more fundamental might seem to devalue them; but let me repeat, memorability was what Saxo tried above all to achieve.

In conclusion, I must define the aim of this paper. It is an attempt to deduce the way Saxo treated the material out of which he constructed the history of his own times, particularly in those areas where there is no reason to suppose that he simply invented it. Inventiveness never deserted him, but in these areas it seems to have been used primarily to produce effective sense-impressions that anchored the narrative in the minds of his readers. These appear most clearly in his anecdotes, descriptions, and images; and it is in the language of these passages, rather than in the intellectual framework of the whole work, that his skill was most exercised. Rather than starting from concepts, and working through the various literary devices towards an exposition of those concepts in history, I see him as beginning with a collection of narratives and then re-fashioning them in the way that would evoke the greatest number of intellectual repercussions. It was here that the art of history, and the art of fiction converged; in the diffraction rather than in the deliberate perversion of the data.

WIT AND ELOQUENCE IN THE COURTS OF SAXO'S EARLY KINGS

HILDA R. ELLIS DAVIDSON

Lucy Cavendish College, University of Cambridge

The work which has recently been done on the writings of Saxo Grammaticus indicates his immense interest in language and learning according to the academic standards of the twelfth century in the universities of western Europe. I want to turn to the other side of the coin: Saxo's keen appreciation of the culture of his own time as expressed in the oral literature of the Scandinavian North. This includes poetic composition, oratory, popular tales and songs, proverbs, riddles and verbal contests in the vernacular, such as he himself must have heard and enjoyed – perhaps even taken part in – in the halls of great men in Denmark. While he often causes his heroes to speak and act as if they were modelled on those of Virgil, they were, after all, breathing a northern air, with their feet firmly set on Danish soil, in a region which had remained outside the domination of Rome. Saxo must have realised long before Hector Chadwick introduced the idea in *The Heroic Age* that there were astonishingly close parallels between the heroic traditions of Rome and those of the North. He claims to have known the *Bjarkamál* in its Danish form, still "recited from memory by many who are conversant with ancient deeds"[1], and whether we accept this statement at its face-value or not, his version of this fine heroic poem, with its stirring appeal to fight on whatever the odds and repay their king for past generosity, defying the fickle war-god who had abandoned them to defeat, is fully in keeping with other surviving poems in the Germanic tradition. If this was indeed recited in Saxo's hearing, then it may be assumed that other poems of this type were still to be heard in Scandinavian halls, and indeed I find it hard to accept that all these ancient poems to which he refers, and of which he made use, had reached him in manuscript form.

In retelling heroic tales, whether from poems or prose sagas, Saxo consciously stressed the parallels with Latin literature, and above all with Virgil. Battles by sea and land, dangerous voyages to supernatural realms, meetings with figures which were more than human, sword duels and stirring appeals to courage, are common to both; his shield-maid Vebiorg, for instance, plays a part in the Battle of Bråvalla in Book VIII which resembles that of the Amazon Camilla in the *Aeneid,* and dies a similar death; gods and godesses appear in disguise and counsel young heroes, like Pallas or Mercury. Saxo has other parallels, as is well known, with situations in other Latin authors: Amleth acts like Brutus in the outwitting of Tarquinius; the set-up at the court of young king Frothi in Book V appears to echo the picture of slaves taking over power in Valerius Maximus[2]; the appearance of Harthgrepa to Hading in Book I and her claim to changing size echoes that of Philosophy to Boethius in the opening of *The Consolation of Philosophy.* Beside many verbal echoes, there are undoubtedly situations modelled on those in the authors whom he admires. Yet it can be established in nearly every case that the situation evoked is a thoroughly northern one, for which parallels can be found which could not have been derived from Virgil or Valerius Maximus. We must assume that Saxo began with careful scrutiny of northern material. Believing, as he tells us in his Preface, that "the Danes of an older age ... alluded in the Roman manner to the splendour of their nobly-wrought achievements", he deliberately chose to emphasise and embellish such incidents as seemed to him to be "in the Roman manner", in order to give dignity and significance to the traditions of his own heroes. He could only do this from a close knowledge of northern literature and traditions, not only from the Icelandic sources, valuable as he found them – as again he assures us in the Preface – but from his own country also, and I believe to a considerable extent from Norway. When we pass from the heroic material to the verbal accomplishments of his heroes, there are striking parallels not only from Icelandic and Germanic written sources, but also from records of entertainment and verbal games and contests in various cultures where the oral tradition is still strong. It seems that Saxo in his early books is frequently echoing the authentic use of the language and wit of his contemporaries, and that he has managed to preserve something of it in his Latin prose and verse. This is no small achievement, although there is little doubt that this double interest has made it difficult for readers of later times, particularly outside Scandinavia, to appreciate some of the material which he has to offer. Yet on the other hand, because he makes use of native traditions with a vigorous life of their own, not confining himself to the highly intellectual, symbolic world of Martianus Capella, or the didactic *exempla* of Valerius Maximus, his early books have continued to hold the interest of many different types of reader, even while they bewildered and puzzled them at certain points.

Saxo uses the device of prose narrative which breaks into verse dialogue in Book I, in the exchanges between Gro, Bess and Gram. Since we do not find examples of this in the later books, although the device of two poems by different speakers set side by side is a favourite one up to Book VIII, it seems that he associates this with the earliest times, when mythological beings took an active part in the careers of northern heroes. In this he is following a well-established tradition, found in a number of poems in the *Poetic Edda* and in the Icelandic legendary sagas, which include meetings with supernatural characters. The first dialogue in particular, in which Gro meets Bess and Gram in disguise, may be set beside one in the Helgi poems, where Atli, a follower of Helgi, exchanges threats and insults with a giantess, Hrimgerðr, and finally Atli is replaced by Helgi himself[3]. Some of the insults are scurrilous and hard to understand; there are references to marriage between Helgi and the giantess, which she evidently desires, but she is rejected, threatened with a loathsome giant for husband, and finally forced to admit that the valkyrie, Svava, has proved stronger than she and has saved Helgi's fleet from destruction. The situation in Saxo is not an exact parallel; indeed it is reversed, since it is the hero and his companions who appear as giants, and have a contest with a princess who resembles a valkyrie, but they prove victorious, and the end is acceptance by Gro of Gram as a husband. It is as though Saxo has used components with which he was familiar and built them up differently, either because he had a different source, one in the same pattern as the Helgi poem, or because he was presenting a poem of his own according to a general rule. There are a considerable number of other examples from Icelandic literature where a god or hero is disguised as a giant or some kind of hooded and unrecognisable stranger[4]. A contest takes place in which boasts and insults and sometimes riddles are exchanged, and finally, when it has been won, the disguise is thrown off and the hero's true identity revealed.

Examples of such contests vary from *Hárbarðsljóð*, where Odin is disguised as a bearded ferryman and defeats Thor after a somewhat crude series of exchanges of an insulting kind, to a more realistic down-to-earth

account of a visit to a Norwegian hall in *Ǫrvar-Odds Saga*. Here Odd visits
the hall calling himself Barkman, with a disguise of birchbark covering
his body and legs and a large hat of the same material to conceal his face.
He takes part in various contests of strength and skill, and finally wins a
drinking bout against two opponents, which as described must have been
a hilarious spectacle for the audience in the hall. Each side has to compose a verse while the other drinks off a horn of ale, which means that
Odd has to drink twice as much as each of the two men opposing him,
and compose twice as many verses. He tells his backer that he is nervous
about this, but he acquits himself well, and is still able to produce unin-
spired but adequate verse, crowing over his opponents and exalting his
own achievements, after they have collapsed helpless on the floor. Soon
after, Odd's disguise is removed and his fine clothes underneath revealed, and he is recognised as the famous champion and traveller from
northern Norway. In studying a number of these encounters in which
boasts and insults are exchanged, as in a Scottish "flyting" of medieval
times, I have come to the conclusion that they are based on various types
of rhyming games, often played between a man and a woman, which was
a favourite pastime in medieval Scandinavia, and may have been particularly popular in Norway[5].

   Such licensed exchange of verbal insult between two people in disguise, or between a disguised visitor and a member of the household, is well
represented in accounts of the practice of house-visiting, a custom still
continuing in fairly remote areas, such as the Danish island of Agersø,
parts of Wales, and Newfoundland. The Agersø material is examined in
an important study by Carsten Bregenhøj, published in 1974[6]; the Welsh
evidence, on which a good deal has been published, is interesting because
it includes the composition of short verses sung by individuals from outside seeking admission to a farm, and replies in the same style and metre
from someone inside[7]; the Newfoundland evidence, edited by Herbert
Halpert and G. M. Story, contains much information about the elaborate
disguises used, among which giant and bird and animal costumes are
frequently found, and for which incidentally birchbark is still used among
other material; it may be noted also that insulting and even obscene
exchanges between men and women who normally behave impeccably
and treat one another with respect and courtesy are characteristic; there
are example also of the disguising of voice by the intake of breath which
makes it hard to recognise the identity and even the sex of the visitor[8].

Thus Saxo's reference to Gram, who "giving a harsher timbre to his voice imitated the hair-raising voice of a giant" becomes more comprehensible, and some knowledge of house-visiting appears to me to offer a possible explanation of some of the more puzzling dialogues in his early books. It may well be that some of them, as Kurt Johannesson claims, had a philosophical significance for Saxo, but he may still have been using material based on native tradition and not be confining himself to purely literary models. I cannot deal here with the many disguise episodes in Saxo, but will only mention one in Book VII, where Oli visits the hall of Prince Thori disguised as an old beggar, with a companion dressed as a woman, both men carrying swords hidden in hollow sticks. He announced that he had been the King of the Beggars in Sivard's court, and been driven out by the king's son. A number of Thori's men, "saluting him by the name of king", says Saxo, "began to kneel to him and offer him their hands for fun." This meant that they pledged him their support, in parody of vows of loyalty made to their real leader, and when he suddenly attacked Thori, a number of them thought this to be part of the fooling, and did not attempt to defend the prince, who was killed in the general confusion. The choosing of a Beggar King and Queen has continued, although in less exalted circles, up to recent times in Denmark, and took place, for instance, not long ago at Egeskov market; Anders Enevig published reminiscenses from individuals who took part in this in 1963[9]. Characters who visited farms in Denmark were often led by an old man known as the Beggar (Stodder) and an old woman (Kælling) who was a man in woman's clothing; these, together with a clown, led the Shrovetide "riding" in North Jutland, for instance, and would request permission to enter the farms and be invited in by the woman of the house.[10] It therefore seems reasonable to suppose that a custom such as Saxo describes was familiar in halls of kings and nobles of his own time.

Customs of this kind gave plenty of scope for wit and eloquence, and those who could conduct verbal exchanges with brilliance as well as mere obscenity would be much in demand. The number of Edda poems and legendary sagas which show the gods themselves, as well as lesser supernatural figures such as giants and dwarfs and troll-women, taking part in such contests suggests that this type of game, rather than more elaborate mythological dramas, such as Bertha Phillpotts claimed, lay behind the dialogue poems of the Poetic Edda[11], may account for the structure of these poems. It would be natural for Saxo to elaborate and dignify such exchanges for his own purposes, as we know he did for the two speeches of Hading and Regnild in Book I, where a short version of eight lines has been preserved in Snorri's *Prose Edda,* represented as a dialogue between the god Njord and his wife Skathi. The subject matter, though not the style, corresponds so closely with Saxo's two poems that there can be little doubt that he was working on a similar source, although we cannot tell whether this was written or oral; like Snorri, he gives no indication of a longer story in which the passage appears. Comparison here is instructive; Saxo has kept to the pattern of the Icelandic, but it would be impossible to reconstruct it from his version; not only has he elaborated it and extended it in a series of complex descriptive phrases, but he has added the idea of a viking longing to return to a life of raiding on the sea to that of the speaker who expressed his preference for the seashore and his dislike of the mountains, thus adapting the speech to the character of a warrior king.

It may be noted that Saxo's long army of heroes in the first eight books are not only men of action and courage, or even prudent and generous rulers who care for the welfare of their people. From Gram onwards, a number of them take part in intellectual pursuits, and these are not restricted to the recital of lays or the making of impressive speeches, important though this aspect may be. Three outstanding heroes to whom Saxo devotes a good deal of attention and apparently greatly admires are Amleth in Book III, Erik the Eloquent in Book V, and Starkather the Old in Books VI and VIII. None of these is a great king; Amleth is the son of a tributary ruler in Jutland, and when he finally wins the throne he does not keep it long; Erik is a Norwegian who took service with King Frothi of Denmark, and Starkather a champion who fought for a number of kings and caused the deaths of two of them by appalling treachery. The link between the three is that while all are brave and adventurous and can find a way out of desperate situations, each is specially distinguished by verbal brilliance and ability to use words in debate, praise, insult, aphorisms or riddling speech. Again parallels for their wit and eloquence can be found, not only in the Icelandic sagas, but also from oral tradition in various parts of the world. It seems to represent the kind of entertainment popular in the halls of kings at a time when written literature was confined to scholars in monasteries and universities. Amleth, the dispossessed prince at his uncle Fengi's court, in great danger because Fengi had killed his father and would remove him if he considered him a real threat, shows his quick wit and subtlety of mind by the answers which he gives to questions, depending on puns, literal interpretation of metaphor, and use of familiar poetic imagery. He is, to some extent, a trickster[12], but the rule he follows is that he must always speak the truth, even though he speaks it in such a way that his hearers misunderstand him. This is closely linked with the riddle game, which we know from surviving examples, such as the collection of riddles in *Hervarar Saga* and the Anglo-Saxon examples in the *Exeter Book,* must have been cultivated in the North. Latin riddles were composed, and no doubt enjoyed in academic circles, but those which survive are far inferior to the brilliant little descriptive poems in the vernacular in the Anglo-Saxon collection or those used by Gestumblindi in his visit to King Heidrek.

When in Book III Amleth replies to the question of whether he has seen a colt after a wolf has passed by, the significance of his words seems at first hard to appreciate: "There are few of that breed", he replies, "in Fengi's stable." Yet Saxo describes his answer as "a moderate but witty criticism which hit at his uncle's affluence." It is not, then, the reply of a simpleton, as the courtiers thought; it is riddling speech of the kind found in skaldic verse and riddling dialogue in the sagas, and is based on the familiar imagery of heroic poetry. The warrior who won victories provided food for the wolves, since he left many dead on the battlefield. Amleth's uncle, the usurper, was no warrior leader, and did not win battles, as his dead brother had done; Fengi had slain this brother, Amleth's father, by treachery, and taken over the wealth which the rightful king had won by valour; therefore indeed there were no wolves in Fengi's stable. In many cases the point of Amleth's remarks, which Saxo carefully quotes, may depend on puns now lost to us, as in the incident of the horse-fly with a straw in its tail, which the court, and no doubt Saxo's contemporaries, found so hilarious. Jørgen Olrik[13] has furnished us with what seems to me a brilliant explanation in unearthing the term *Avnebag* (straw-buttocks) used of a thief who conceals gleanings from his neighbours' fields in his baggy trousers; this would mean that the fly was a warning to Amleth that the king's men were on the watch and that he must be as cautious as the thief in concealing what he was about. Finally in the episode of the burning hall and the hooks which fasten down the tapestries, like a great salmon-net, we have imagery which belongs to the Trickster tradition in the North and shows Amleth acting with the cunning of Loki the Arch-Trickster, who also invented a net to be burnt in the fire. Saxo's excessive praise of Amleth at the end of Book III, in words warmer than those applied to any other hero, shows how the mixture of courage and fortitude with subtlety and skill over words appealed to him; and this combination is hardly a conventional one among the qualities of kings.

Secondly we have Erik, the young Norwegian; and why, it may be asked, did Saxo pay so much attention to a hero from Norway in a history of Danish kings, showing Erik many times outwitting and triumphing over the Danes? Was it because he felt that in his story there were resemblances to Absalon in his work as counsellor and partner to King Valdemar? Or because the types of eloquence for which Erik won the title of *Disertus* were particularly cultivated in Norway? Whatever the reason, Erik arrives at the court of Frothi with his fosterbrother, desiring service with the young king, and finds him surrounded by a villainous group of thugs, bullies and degenerate courtiers. The court already possesses an expert in verbal skills, a middle-aged woman called Gøtvar, but Erik has little trouble in outdoing her, and ultimately takes her place. She had previously been sent abroad as diplomatic representative to arrange a royal marriage, but after Erik defeated her in a public contest it was he who was responsible for missions abroad, like that to the king of Norway to propose a marriage between Frothi and his daughter, and the visit to the King of the Huns. The contest between Gøtvar and Erik is of some interest; she is the challenger, and wagers a valuable neck ornament that she can defeat him in the making of verse; she then produces two lines of such obscenity that Elton refused to translate them. Unperturbed, Erik replies with six lines in similar metre, even more outspoken, giving a reply from the male point of view. Saxo gives us a glimpse here of what must have formed a popular type of entertainment, and the clue to understanding it can be found in parallels elsewhere. There is a contest with exchange of verses included in two manuscripts of the *Prose Edda*[14], represented as taking place between the Norwegian poet Bragi, who lived in the mid-ninth century, and a troll-women. She challenged him to reply to a verse which begins "I am called Troll", and consists of a series of kennings, or roundabout ways of saying this; he replied with a verse beginning "I am called Skald", which continues similarly with a series of kennings for poet. The point of the game is evidently for the challenger to speak a verse in a certain metre and style, and for the opponent to cap this, using the same style and keeping to the given subject; the audience

then decides who is the winner. Outspoken verse of the kind Gøtvar
produced was no doubt familiar in contests between men and women,
and it is hardly surprising that it is not often recorded; we have a partial
example in *Grettis Saga*[15] when a maidservant discovers Grettir sleeping
naked in the hall after a swim and taunts him, and he speaks two verses in
reply. There are also riddles in the *Exeter Book* which bear some resemblance to Gøtvar's lines, since they contain double entendre of the battle-
axe and whetstone type[16]; comparison might also be made with the
riddle about the horse and mare in *Hervarar Saga*[17]. Parallels have also
been suggested with Swedish rhyming games which were popular as late
as the eighteenth century[18].

Erik distinguishes himself in other ways; when sent to view the army of
the Huns, he utters a challenge in formal rhetoric and each side boasts of
coming victory. He also engages in an elaborate series of riddles when he
meets the Danish king, presenting his credentials, as it were, in reply to
the command:

"You, the one who indulges himself in haughty language and a decora-
tive display of style, tell us your place of departure and your reason for
coming here."

Erik's answers are cryptic, like those of Amleth, and belong to the
riddling tradition; he appears to use place-names, farm names and personal names, giving them a literal interpretation, and also, like Amleth,
heroic imagery. In one case he declares:

"As I was resting there, a pack of wolves, glutted with human corpses,
came and licked the points of my weapons. Then the tip of the king's
spear was shaken off, that is to say, Fridlef's grandson."

Fridlef is utterly mystified, as the modern reader may well be: "You've
quite baffled my understanding with your dark riddles", he admits. Erik
then gives a partial explanation: "My mention of the spear point just now
signified the slaying of Odd by my own hand." Odd's name means the
point of a weapon, and the wolves who licked it are the same wolves
known to Amleth, who are fed by warriors when they devour the slain
after a battle; Odd was apparently related to the king, since they had the
same grandfather. This kind of wit has by no means disappeared; it is
familiar to the crossword puzzle enthusiast, particularly the kind of puzzle which depends on fantastic word-play.

Finally, Erik is also an expert on proverbs, and is much admired for
this skill; a large number of proverbs and aphorisms are introduced in

Book V. Saxo would of course know Latin and Biblical parallels, since proverbs are universal, but the way in which Erik's use of them is acknowledged as apt and unanswerable is evidently part of the oral tradition, and of his special gift of eloquence. We have a long series of gnomic utterances in the brilliant poem or group of poems in the *Edda,* known as *Hávamál,* thought by many to have been composed in Norway, and some of these can be compared with Erik's examples. When he refers, for instance, to the Danes' preparations for war in his meeting with the King of the Huns, who is planning to attack them, he declares:

"Frothi never waits at home, lingering in his halls, for a hostile army ... Nobody has ever won victory by snoring, nor has any sleeping wolf found a carcase."

The king, we are told, "immediately recognised his intelligence from these carefully chosen apothegms." The one quoted can be compared directly with lines from *Hávamál:*

A man should be up early, if he wishes to take
    the life or wealth of another;
the wolf snug in his lair never gets a bite at the leg,
    nor does the sleeping man gain a victory.

It appears from Saxo's account that there is immediate appreciation and acknowledgement of an apt saying. Grep, one of the leading bullies of the court, challenged Erik on his arrival and poured abuse at him, calling him fool and rascal, lowborn buffoon and night-owl, who should be made a feast for the crows. Erik simply took the exchange on to a higher plane, replying by gnomic utterances of the *Hávamál* type, and at this Grep acknowledged defeat; he realised that he could not compete in this type of debate, and moreover Erik goaded him into defending himself in direct speech, which meant that he had lost the game. He was by no means philosophical about it:

"When he reached home, he filled the palace with a tempestuous fit of yells, and shouting that he had been defeated, urged all his warriors to gather their weapons, intending to avenge his misfortunes in the vocal contest by force."

This same skill saved Erik from death on another occasion, when the Hunnish king accused him of spying, and then recognised him as the man who had declared his daughter (Frothi's wife) guilty of adultery. He ordered his men to bind Erik, but Erik replied that it was unfitting for one man to be overcome by many, a saying which had been used by Saxo earlier[19]. It was evidently a recognised aphorism, and the king immediately let him go free. The inspiration for this episode seems to come from the Icelandic poem on the *Battle of the Goths and Huns,* which Saxo draws on more than once[20]. Here an unknown messenger who brings a challenge to the Huns is to be put to death, but the king intervenes with the words: "We must not harm messengers who travel alone." However, as Saxo uses it, it appears to be the right saying produced at the right moment which is Erik's trump card, acknowledged by his enemies. Erik's long speech to dissuade the king from suicide is a more conventional use of debate in the academic manner. But he proved himself just as adept at what might have seemed to scholars popular and frivolous types of debating, while he also showed himself a master of magic in his use of a horse's head against the Danish sorcerers[21], and outwitted those who sought to overcome him in crude tests of physical strength, evidently popular in Danish society, such as pulling a skin from under his feet, or setting him to pull on a ring of rope, or to fight on ice.[22] In fact here, as so often in the early books, traditional skills are mingled with the new training in thought and language, and Saxo throws himself with enthusiasm into both aspects of his chosen hero, whose versatility echoes his own.

Thirdly we have the character of Starkather, one of the most memorable of Saxo's heroes, who like Amleth has possible mythological associations. He is a man of enormous courage and endurance, a dedicated warrior refusing to give up the rigours of military life, and a constant reminder to Danish princes and princesses of their duties and responsibilities. Like the grimmer prophets of the Old Testament, he had no mercy on human weaknesses; he condemned the luxuries of the Danish court, and showed himself a firm believer in the obligations demanded from each class of society, and the necessity of remaining in one's own niche. The grim giant champion, whose fame was remembered in many countries round the Baltic, does not seem outside Saxo to have acted as a moralist and satirist as he does in Books VI and VIII. He was celebrated as a poet, but we are told in one of the Icelandic stories about him that Thor decreed that he would never be able to remember the poems he composed. Poems represented as his in Icelandic sources are relatively late in date.[23] Karsten Friis-Jensen has given good reasons for thinking that his long satiric attacks in Book VI are Saxo's own work, modelled on classical satire, and that this portion of the *History* is a "skald's saga in Latin."[24] It is an arresting idea if we can indeed view this poet as the prototype of a line of skalds in the Icelandic Family Sagas who are quarrelsome, bold and tactless, unlucky in their dealings with women, ready with abusive language, capable of regrettable and even base actions, and described as dark and ugly, with troll-like characteristics. Men like Kormak and Gunnlaug, Hallfred, Bjorn of Hitsdale and Skarphedin, and even the great master Egil Skallagrimsson himself, share to some extent this type of character. We know also from the work of Bo Almqvist[25] the importance of vindictive, insulting, satirical verses in Icelandic tradition, and from poems of Egil composed in Norway[26] how a man with a gift for biting words can trounce a host who has not received him with the proper welcome and courtesy. Thus once more it seems that Saxo has combined the use of language – this time, used satirically – in the classical manner with the rich traditions of his own background and the verbal skills of the North. The realistic little pictures which slip into Starkather's poetry, not only the elaborate descriptions of roast meats, vegetables and sausages, shellfish and bowls of cream, but the glimpses he gives of the cowman playing his pipe and the scullions stealthily dipping their crusts into the soup they are preparing for their masters, bring us back to the familiar world, and are not part of a slavish imitation of literary models. Starkather, for all his strong convictions concerning duty and discipline, never ceases to be a creature of the barbarous North.

My main point then is that the detailed dependence of Saxo on northern sources and native oral tradition becomes increasingly apparent in studying the earlier books. When in the Preface he speaks of the genius of the early Danes, who told of the feats of their ancestors in runic inscriptions and in songs of their mother tongue, I believe that this is no conventional gesture, like Geoffrey of Monmouth's references to lost sources. There is a sincerity here, which, together with the toughness and realism of many of his episodes, gives a strength and vitality to the stories of the early books which has endeared them to many readers, for all their strangeness. For all his enthusiasm and awareness of classical models and the new learning of his time, Saxo did not despise his own antecedents. If only those early Danes, he laments, could have known Latin, so that their records were not limited to their own ancient tongue. Part of the urge behind these rich and crowded books was the knowledge that he, equipped with an understanding of Latin which few in the North could equal, was capable of rescuing these works from oblivion, encouraged no doubt by the achievements of the Icelanders, and the wealth of stories which they were preserving from a pagan past. In doing this, he has shown himself expert in the craft of the spoken word and of verbal games and contests as well as that of grammar and historical theory, and he has risked the misunderstanding of posterity. But the calling of a Saxo colloquium in 1979 indicates that he has not wholly lost the game.

[1] The version used here and throughout is from Peter Fisher's translation of the first nine books of Saxo to be published with my commentary (SAXO GRAMMATICUS. *The history of the Danes. Books I-IX*. Transl. by Peter Fisher. Ed. with a commentary by Hilda Ellis Davidson, 2 vols., Cambridge 1979-80, vol. 1 p. 63).

[2] VALERIUS MAXIMUS 9,1,2 in the description of the city of Volsinum when slaves gained control.

[3] *Helgakviða Hjǫrvarðssonar*, verses 12 ff.

[4] I have discussed these in detail in a paper on 'Insults and riddles in the Edda poems' to be published in *Edda. A collection of essays* (University of Manitoba Icelandic Series, 4).

[5] Detailed accounts of such practices are represented as taking place in Norway during the journeys of saga heroes, e.g. *Egils saga* 44; *Ǫrvar-Odds saga* 24, or possibly in Scania (*Egils saga* 48); Hávamál, with its many allusions to behaviour in the hall and its wealth of aphorisms, is thought to have originated in Norway rather than Iceland (E. WESSÉN. 'Havamal. Några stilfrågor', *Filologiskt arkiv* vol. 8 (1959) p. 11ff.).

[6] CARSTEN BREGENHØJ. *Helligtrekongersløb på Agersø*, København 1974 (Dansk Folkemindesamling. Skrifter, 3).

[7] TREFOR M. OWEN. *Welsh folk customs*, National Museum of Wales, Cardiff 1974, pp. 51-58, 163-167.

[8] HERBERT HALPERT and G.M. STORY (eds.), *Christmas mumming in Newfoundland*, Toronto 1969; see especially p. 148ff.; 209ff.

[9] ANDERS ENEVIG. *Prinser og vagabonder*, København 1963, p. 16ff.; 38ff.

[10] J.S. MØLLER. *Fester og Højtider i gamle Dage*, vol. 2, Holbæk 1933, p. 19ff.

[11] B.S. PHILLPOTTS. *The elder Edda and ancient Scandinavian drama*, Cambridge 1920.

[12] H.R. ELLIS DAVIDSON. 'Loki and Saxo's Hamlet', *The fool and the trickster. Studies in honour of Enid Welsford*. Ed. by P.V.A. Williams, Cambridge 1979, pp. 3-17.

[13] JØRGEN OLRIK. 'Avnebag. Forklaring til en Gaade i Amled-Sagnet', *Festskrift til H.F. Feilberg*, København 1911, pp. 98-100.

[14] SNORRI STURLUSON. *Edda*. Udg. af Finnur Jónsson, København 1926², Skálds. 51. The trollwoman's poem, found in two MSS only, is given in a note, p. 126. See BO ALMQVIST. *Norrön niddiktning*, vol. 1, Uppsala 1965 (Nordiska texter och undersökningar, 21), p. 28ff.

[15] *Grettis saga* 75.

[16] C. WILLIAMSON. *The Old English riddles of the Exeter Book*, Chapel Hill 1977. See riddles 42 (Key), 43 (Dough), 52 (Churn), 59 (Helmet/Shirt).

[17] *The Saga of King Heidrek the Wise*. Transl. with introduction, notes and appendices by Christopher Tolkien, London 1960 (Icelandic Texts), Appendix pp. 81-82. The riddle is found in the H text only.

[18] JOSEF SVENNUNG, 'Eriks und Götvaras Wortstreit bei Saxo', *Arkiv för nordisk filologi* vol. 56 (1942) p. 88ff. I owe this reference to Inge Skovgaard-Petersen.

[19] Book V (OR p. 114): »It was improper for a few men to be attacked by a great swarm«.

[20] For example, in the description of the vast army of the Huns.

[21] ALMQVIST (note 14 above) discusses the rite (also used by the hero in *Egils saga)* p. 100ff.

[22] For *dra hank* and other amusements of this kind popular in medieval Scandinavia, see J. GÖTLIND, 'Idrotter och friluftslekar', *Nordisk Kultur* vol. 24 (1933) p. 21ff.

[23] For the difficult problem of the Starkad sources, see JAN DE VRIES, 'Die Starkadsage', *Germanisch-romanische Monatsschrift* vol. 36 (1955) pp. 281-297.

[24] In a paper given at Cambridge in 1978 and in another included in this volume.

[25] See note 14 above.

[26] *Egils saga* 44.

ON TRANSLATING SAXO INTO ENGLISH[1]

PETER FISHER

Cambridgeshire College of Arts and Technology

I should like to begin by saying something about my distinguished predecessor in the work of translating the first nine books of Saxo Grammaticus into English, Professor Oliver Elton, whose version appeared in
1894.[2] In his biography of Frederick York Powell[3] he is mainly concerned
to convey the inspiration Powell gave him and show his industry in compiling the introduction on sources, historical methods and folk-lore, but
in doing so he reveals something about his own practices and views on
translating Saxo. Starting sometime after April 1889, Elton would send
each batch of material to his friend for scrutiny, and would receive a
sheet of comments and emendations by return of post, which helped the
translation "to a greater correctness and to a better language and caden-
ce". He calls the work "a laborious affair, which took the leisure of a few
years", remarking that Saxo's Latin is "rhetorical and inflated but often
sharply picturesque", and at the same time "odd and full of traps". I have
often had cause for sympathy with Elton's words, though I must immediately add that the business of translating Saxo has also given me enormous pleasure.

Though in the introduction to his translation he pays tribute to the
resource and strength of Saxo's style, what Elton terms the "quaint, half-
pedantic effect" of the Latin is, to a certain extent, aimed at in his
rendering. Hence the "doth's" and "thou's" in the speeches and aphorisms, like William Morris's versions of Icelandic sagas, are consistent
with the Victorian taste for archaism, but now sound old-fashioned and
stilted. None the less Elton, who took First-class Honours in *Literae
humaniores* at Oxford, was no mean classical scholar, and his work,
despite its eighty-six years, still reads well, maintaining a high degree of
accuracy. For the one or two rare occasions when I have been able to
fault him, he has set me right many times. It is a testament to the endu-

ringness of his efforts that, to the best of my knowledge, no other translation has been used in the numerous English works which have quoted
sections from the *Gesta Danorum*.

My own view is that "a quaint, half-pedantic effect" represents a rather
narrow conception of Saxo's style, for his range is much wider than this.
For me the main criterion must be readability. As Ronald Knox once
pointed out, a translation is meant for the reader who either lacks the
skill or the opportunity to read the original, so that he may expect the
same interest and enjoyment as he would from the original. The first
quality of a book must be that people wish to read it and go on reading it.
By its nature Latin lends itself to long periods and when Saxo, following
such intricate models as Martianus Capella, extends these to several
lines, the translator needs to chop up his sentences, while still trying to
preserve something of their elegant variation and balance. Here is an
example:

> Quibus auditis, Haldanus, ut erat circa piraticam occupatus, expe-
> dire militibus dixit, ut, qui in exteros hactenus desaevierint, nunc
> civium visceribus ferrum adigant ereptique regni iniuriam propul-
> sent, qui dilatandi curam gerere consueverint. (185,21).[4]
>
> *As soon as he heard of this revolt, Haldan, there and then in the*
> *middle of a pirating expedition, told his soldiers to arm themselves*
> *for battle. Though they had hitherto savaged foreigners, they must*
> *now drive their swords into the bowels of their own countrymen;*
> *whereas they were usually bent on extending the empire, they must*
> *now avert its unlawful theft.*

Nevertheless, while simplifying some of Saxo's syntactical effects in the
interests of a more flexible English prose, it is important to keep the
flavour of the original. On first consulting Saxo's Latin, anyone must
inevitably be struck by his immense wealth of vocabulary, a stylistic
feature testified by Franz Blatt's admirable and comprehensive glossary
in the Copenhagen edition; the translator must therefore exert himself to
use the utmost resources of his own language.

Thirdly, there is a certain dignity in the Latin which must not be
allowed to become too colloquial in the attempt to render the original
into modern English idiom. Faced with the word *sponsus*, it is obviously
better to opt for the slightly older equivalent "betrothed", than the nor-

mal present-day "fiancé". On the other hand, to avoid a certain stiffness of expression in conversations, it is preferable to use the short "I'll" or "won't", etc. instead of their unabbreviated forms.

As an illustration of straightforward narrative, where Saxo is chiefly concerned to move on his story, I choose a passage from the tale of Asmund and Asvith, the account of the man who returns from the dead like a vampire to persecute the friend who has chosen to be incarcerated alive in his tomb.

Inter haec Asuithus morbo consumptus cum cane ac equo terreno mandatur antro. Cum quo Asmundus ob amicitiae iusiurandum vivus contumulari sustinuit, cibo quo vesceretur illato. Iamque Ericus cum exercitu superiora permensus Asuithi forte tumulum appetebat; cui Sueones thesauros inesse rati ligonibus perfregere collem. Itaque maioris quam credebatur altitudinis specum aperiri conspiciunt. Ad quem perlustrandum opus erat eo, qui se in illum pendulo circumligatum fune demitteret. Delectus est sorte ex promptissimis iuvenibus unus; quem cum Asmundus sporta restim sequente intromissum aspiceret, protinus, eiecto eo, corbem conscendit. Deinde superne astantibus ac moderantibus funem abstrahendi signum porrexit. Qui ingentis pecuniae spe reducto corbe, cum ignotam extracti speciem animadverterent, inusitata facie territi defunctumque redisse rati, proiecta reste, in diversa fugere. (Book V; 135, 30-136,2)

Meanwhile Asvith died from an illness and was committed with his horse and dog to a cavern in the earth. Because of their oath of friendship Asmund suffered himself to be buried alive with him and food was put inside for him to eat. Erik, who had crossed the highlands with his army, now chanced to come near Asvith's tomb, and, since the Swedes believed that it contained treasure, they broke into the hillside with their mattocks, only to perceive that they had opened up a cave of greater depth than they had anticipated. Its exploration required someone to be let down into space tied to the end of a rope. One of the spryest of the young men was chosen by lot for the purpose. When Asmund caught sight of him being sent down in a basket attached to a cord, he immediately tumbled him out, climbed into the basket himself and gave a signal for those who were standing above, controlling the rope, to haul him up. They drew up the basket

expecting a pile of money and were aghast at the extraordinary sight
of the unknown man they had pulled out; thinking the dead had
returned to life, they flung away the rope, and shot off in all direc-
tions.

Here, unusually, I have combined some of Saxo's shortish sentences to
give more smoothness and continuity in English. His trick of *interpreta-*
tio, expressing the same thought in different words, is difficult to handle,
and often has to appear more simply in English; thus, here, *ignotam*
speciem ... inusitata facie is rendered by "the extraordinary sight of the
unknown man". I have sought to employ vivid, graphic vocabulary to
carry over the excitement of Saxo's story, hence "let down into space"
(pendulo fune demitterent), "spryest" *(promptissimis),* "shot off in all
directions" *(in diversa fugere).*

Greater difficulties arise in conveying the effect of heavily rhetorical
passages, like the long speeches between Erik and Frothi in Book Five,
when the latter has been rescued from drowning. Hence one has no
option but to swallow prejudices and to translate fairly literally, even if
verisimilitude is sacrificed. At the beginning of Ulvild's haughty speech
to her husband towards the end of Book One, I have tried to reproduce
the effect of Saxo's highly patterned language:

O miseram me, cuius nobilitatem dispar copulae nexus obtenebrat!
O infelicem, cuius stemmati rustica iugatur humilitas! O infortuna-
tam principis prolem, quam tori lege plebeius aequiparat! Miseran-
dam regis filiam, cuius decorem ignavus pater in obsoletos ac despi-
cabiles transmisit amplexus! Infaustam matris subolem, cuius felici-
tati tori commercium derogat, cuius munditiam immunditia ruralis
attrectat, dignitatem indignitas vulgaris inclinat, ingenuitatem con-
dicio maritalis extenuat! (33,38-34,6)

I am wretched because my dignity is obscured by an ill-fitting
bond, distressed that my lineage is yoked to base peasantry. Unblest
is the child of royalty whom the law of wedlock levels with the mob;
pitiful the king's daughter whose father has idly transferred her ele-
gance to low and contemptible embraces; ill-starred the mother's
offspring whose happiness is diminished by her wedded partner,
whose purity is handled by yokel filth (munditiam immunditia),
whose nobility is demeaned to ignoble vulgarity (dignitatem indignitas), *whose value dwindles in the married state.*

Saxo often cultivates paronomasia, plays on words, as one of his rhetorical devices, and this one must try to find parallels for. Here, for instance, from Book Seven, is a description of the warlike company of women led by Alvild:

> Hae ergo, perinde ac nativae condicionis immemores rigoremque blanditiis anteferentes, bella pro basiis intentabant sanguinemque, non oscula delibantes armorum potius quam amorum officia frequentabant manusque, quas in telas aptare debuerant, telorum obsequiis exhibebant, ut iam non lecto, sed leto studentes spiculis appeterent, quos mulcere specie potuissent. (192,21-6)
>
> *As if they were forgetful of their true selves, they put toughness before allure, aimed at conflicts instead of kisses, tasted blood, not lips, sought the clash of arms rather than the arm's embrace, fitted to weapons hands which should have been weaving, desired not the couch but the kill, and those they could have appeased with looks they attacked with lances.*

An attempt has been made to transfer the contrived effect of the Latin by strong alliteration and occasional puns. (Those who are curious may like to compare Elton's version of this passage, where he employs the same techniques.) The danger is of producing something so odd that it will arrest and puzzle the reader. Most difficult of all, perhaps, are the quips and riddles of the trickster characters, like Amleth or Erik, where one must imply a hidden meaning beneath obscurity. All too often the hidden meaning is itself obscure.

I feel strongly that Saxo's verse passages should be rendered in verse, following the lead of such earlier translators as Herrmann and Olrik. Saxo, while not always an inspired poet, is a good metrist, and these sections should stand out as strikingly from the surrounding prose as they do in the Latin text. I have avoided trying to write hexameters or pentameters, which, despite the experiments of Tennyson and others, read rather clumsily in English, but have in each case chosen a line of roughly equivalent length to the original. Normally, though not quite always, I have followed the tradition of putting Latin hexameters into blank verse, and at all times have marched with current taste in eschewing rhyme. Every translator works within the conventions of his own age, and had I lived in the early eighteenth century, Saxo's hexameters or elegiacs would automatically have been turned into rhymed heroic couplets. Where a metrical line can be put over without much difficulty by an exactly equivalent rhythm in English, I have gladly used it, as with adonics, whether alone, as in the exchange between Gro and Bess in Book One, or as part of the more common sapphic stanza. The trochaic tetrameter catalectic, a metre used by Julius Caesar's soldiers for scurrilous verses on their leader as they escorted him in his Gallic triumph, goes naturally into English too. The corpse which is compelled to speak by the giantess Harthgrepa has the refrain:

> Inferis me qui retraxit, exsecrandus oppetat
> Tartaroque devocati spiritus poenas luat. (22,25)

This becomes:

> *Let the one who summoned me, a spirit from the underworld,*
> *dragged me from the infernal depths, be cursed and perish*
> > *miserably.*

Rather than reflect the *oppetat-luat* rhyme in the line endings, I have preferred here to let the assonance of "me" and "miserably" give an incantatory ring to the couplet.

While remembering as a warning the definition of poetry as "that which is lost in translation", I have generally taken more licence in the verse passages and aimed at a colourful and stylish idiom rather than complete literalness. Having established a clear number of beats in a line, I have been relatively free with the number of syllables to a foot, and also, in the interests of fluidity, have tended to avoid sequences of end-stopped lines, even where they occur in the Latin, since these can sound monotonous in English. Here is a specimen taken from the sapphics delivered by Starkather, when he is belabouring King Ingel for his epicurean dissoluteness. Since the poem appears to have affinities with classical satire, I have thought it occasionally appropriate to introduce a vulgar word:

> Non ego magnum memini Frothonem
> dexteram fibris volucrum dedisse,
> podicem cocti lacerasse galli
> > pollice curvo.

Quis prior regum potuit gulosus
viscerum putres agitare sordes
aut manu carptim fodicare foedum
    alitis anum?

Fortium crudus cibus est virorum,
nec reor lautis opus esse mensis,
mens quibus belli meditatur usum
    pectore forti.

Aptius barbam poteras rigentem
mordicus presso lacerare dente
quam vorax lactis vacuare sinum
    ore capaci.

Fugimus lautae vitium popinae,
rancidis ventrem dapibus foventes;
coctiles paucis placuere suci
    tempore prisco.

Discus herbosi vacuus saporis
arietum carnes dabat et suillas;
temperans usus nihil immodesto
    polluit ausu.   (173,33)

I never recall the great Frothi
digging his right hand inside a fowl,
tearing at the rump of a roast chicken
    with crooked thumb.

What previous king was ever such a
gourmand as to rummage in unclean, rotten
entrails, scoop and claw with his fist at
    a filthy bird's arse?

Valiant men eat raw rations.
No need of a sumptuous spread, I think,
for stout-hearted bosoms which meditate
    the practice of war.

You might more fittingly sink your teeth
in your bristly beard, bite and rend it,
than greedily drain that bowl of cream
*   with your wide-open mouth.*

I have shunned the taint of this lavish cook-shop,
staying my appetite with rancid fare.
Few were delighted in times gone by
*   with hot sauces,*

when a plate of ram's and swine's flesh was
provided, without any taste of herbs;
through sparing habits no man was defiled
*   by immoderation.*

Verbs like "digging", "tearing", "rummage", "scoop and claw", "bite and rend" are used to give the necessary vigour to the passage, where sometimes Saxo uses a more neutral word, e.g. "digging" for *dedisse;* for the same reason *lactis* is translated "cream" rather than "milk", since the whole tenor of the poem is to accentuate Ingel's gluttony.

I am convinced that Saxo had a good sense of humour, a characteristic not always obvious in some of the earlier translations, where the mood is uniformly serious. It is clear that Saxo takes great enjoyment in Erik's or Amleth's quibbles and extraordinary behaviour. An amused contempt emerges when he is describing the antics of the self-styled gods, whom Saxo, following the current scholarly explanations of euhemerism, takes to be human impostors, with sufficient legerdemain to pass themselves off as supernatural beings. In particular, when he is relating Odin's wooing of Rind, on whom he is hoping to get a son to avenge the death of Balder, there is a delighted gusto in his telling of her repulses, which must be conveyed by a lighter tone than elsewhere. *Cuius benignissimo favore recreatus, dum a puella osculum peteret, alapam recepit* (70,19) becomes: "Uplifted by [the king's] friendly encouragement, he tried to kiss the girl and was rewarded with a slap across the face." (*Alapa*, besides being biblical, has associations with the satire of Juvenal and Martial.) Similarly, *Quem Rinda basium sibi porrigere cupientem colapho percussit* translates easily into "Whenever he wished to offer her a kiss, she boxed his ears" (*colaphus* is a favourite word in Roman comedy). On his third attempt Odin is even more unfortunate: *Quam cum discessurus osculo petere vellet, ita ab ea propulsus est, ut mentum terrae nutabundus impingeret:* "When, on one occasion, just before departing, he wanted to snatch a kiss from her, she gave him such a shove that he was sent flying and banged his chin on the floor." Saxo clearly relished Odin's discomfort.

The names of Saxo's characters present a severe problem for the translator. The Latin forms look out-of-place for Viking heroes, and equally Olrik's updated Danish forms seem wrong for a medieval author. Knudsen, Kristensen and Hornby's *Danmarks gamle Personnavne*[5] gave a great deal of help, but my colleague, Hilda Davidson, and I finally made the decision to adhere as closely as possible to Saxo's spelling, and to be guided only in the terminations by the dictionary of proper names. Thus "Bemoni" is given for *Bemonus,* "Gunnild" for *Gunnilda.* The letter *w* has been changed to *v, I* altered to *J* for the initial consonant, and where a historical character was already familiar in an English spelling, this has been retained, e.g. Charles for *Karolus* when this refers to Charlemagne. (There is another *Karolus* mentioned at the beginning of Book Seven, governor of Götaland, who becomes Karl.) Such has been our system for transferring personal name forms, but no rule-of-thumb covers all, and in some cases it seemed preferable to keep Saxo's own spelling in its entirety. Amleth's mother remains Gerutha rather than Gerthrud, a version nearer to Shakespeare's but somewhat distant from Saxo's form. She is Geruth in *The Historie of Hamblet* of 1608, an English translation of Belleforest, but the final *–a* serves to distinguish her from Geruth *(Geruthus),* the mysterious giant in Book Eight. Sometimes Saxo's form seemed preferable merely on the grounds of euphony, hence Svanloga rather than Svanløgh, the ending given in the Danish volume of old personal names. Tribes have generally been Anglicized to conform with the above, so that the English version speaks of Thronds and Estlanders rather than Throndi and Estones. Accepted spellings like "Alemanni" have, however, been retained.

The rationale for place names has been to employ the modern equivalent, where the name still exists in a similar, recognizable form. So, Blekinge for *Blekingia,* Hälsingland for *Helsingia.* On the other hand, where names have now changed completely, as has so often happened in countries within the Soviet bloc, Saxo's form has been retained. Otherwise Duna, in modern Latvia, would have to be changed to Daugavpils,

Rotala in Estonia into Haapsalu. However, where an accepted medieval form is in use to refer to certain provinces of early times, this has been incorporated. Scania, therefore, is used in preference to present-day Skåne, and Saxo's *Gothia* is rendered by Götaland. In certain cases, of course, the modern names of countries are misleading, and this has had to be indicated where necessary in the commentary. Russia is one instance, where Saxo would have understood only a rather limited area, east and south-east of Estland and Kurland, stretching not much further east than Moscow.

I have tried to locate on maps every place referred to by Saxo, with something like ninety per cent success. Certain names have constantly defeated identification, as, for example, the Bøcherør in Sweden, which is named as a rendezvous by Snio and the king of Götaland's daughter in Book Eight. Once, a name appears to have been totally misplaced by Saxo, his *Campus Laneus,* presumably a Latinization of Ullar-akr, which he puts near the coast of Scania, though Snorri's *Heimskringla* clearly indicates that it lies just outside Uppsala.[6]

Stephanius[7] has given some guidance on a few linguistic points, especially where his commentary is at its fullest, near the beginning of the work. His explanation of *negotium intorsit* in the seventh line of the Preface, for example, in which he rightly points out that the metaphor is taken from the launching of a weapon by an enemy and always implies a certain violence, led to the rendering: "the labour was thrown upon me". In line 22 on the same page, his note on *tanti cognitoris praesidio,* where he reminds the reader that *cognitor* is properly a legal term, influenced the resulting phrase: "with your strong protection and advocacy". Indeed, his remarks are always full of common-sense and still often a useful corrective when interpretation in uncertain. There are some passages, however, which neither Stephanius nor any later commentator has hitherto managed to elucidate successfully. Such is the notorious account of the military formation explained by Odin to King Harald in Book Seven (207,30-208,10), of which Herrmann remarks sadly: "vieles bleibt unsicher oder ganz dunkel".[8]

There is a poem near the opening of Book Two, within which Saxo has incorporated a series of names straight out of Martianus Capella, in order to embellish his account of the supernatural terrors which invest the princes Regner and Thorald at the instigation of their stepmother:

Trux Lemurum chorus advehitur, praecepsque per auras
cursitat et vastos edit ad astra sonos.
Accedunt Fauni Satyris, Panumque caterva
Manibus admixta militat ore fero;
Silvanis coeunt Aquili, Larvaeque nocentes
cum Lamiis callem participare student.
Saltu librantur Furiae, glomerantur iisdem
Fanae, quas Simis Fantua iuncta premit. (39,37-40,6)

Lemures, fauns and satyrs, *manes, larvae, lamiae,* and *furiae* are all well-attested and explained in classical sources, and *Simi* must surely resemble monkeys, but there are difficulties with the unusual names *Fanae, Fantua* and *Aquili.* The translator has a choice here of leaving these obscure words as they are, or trying to wrest some meaning out of them. Du Cange helps a very little, but rather better aid is provided by the ninth-century commentator on Martianus, Remigius of Auxerre.[9] *Fana,* according to Remigius, are the replies given by evil spirits in temples; *Fatuae* (or *Fantua*), spirits who drive men mad or make them *energuminos,* possessed of the devil, though Fatua occurs also as the sister of the prophetic god Faunus, a name which in medieval Latin can signify an evil spirit. *Aquilus,* says Remigius, is a type of demon which appears in the form of an eagle, with a curved beak. The word is repeated in Book Eight when Thorkil meets two such monsters and refers rather rudely to their inelegant noses (244,36). The four elegiac couplets, now stripped of their proper names, turn out like this:

A savage choir of spectres hurtle along the wind,
raising their deafening howl to the stars.
Satyrs and fauns, horned and hoofed, with wrathful
gaze fight alongside the ghosts.
Here too flock bird-headed fiends pressing their way,
deadly ghouls and witches together,
furies bound forward, with them devil-gods thronging,
jostled by the hell-hag and baboon-faced demons.

Having outlined some of the problems, and I hope too the pleasures, of translating Saxo into English, let me end by quoting some remarks of

Richmond Lattimore, the accomplished American translator of ancient Greek drama. "The translator, if he is human, will deal with most problems as he meets them. His principles will come out later, by way of self-explanation, or self-defence."[10] My own experience has been exactly this; rather than start with a series of pre-conceptions (such as that Saxo needs to be rendered with "a quaint, half-pedantic effect"), the translator finds a style to suit his author as he goes along, and devises answers to the various difficulties as he encounters them. Only at this much later stage of self-justification does he rationalize his methods. Lattimore goes on to observe that a translation, in particular a verse translation, will be a product of author and translator, not merely a sum of the two. The original works, however, are indestructible, whereas, with the passage of time, one translation after another will become an antique. Professor Elton's version of Saxo has stood the test of over eighty years and still retains a great deal of vitality for the contemporary reader; any modern translation of this author which can last even half as long before it is inevitably superseded will have been remarkably successful.

[1] SAXO GRAMMATICUS. *The history of the Danes. Books I-IX.* Transl. by Peter Fisher. Ed. with a commentary by Hilda Ellis Davidson, 2 vols., Cambridge 1979-80.

[2] *The first nine books of the Danish history of Saxo Grammaticus.* Transl. by Oliver Elton. With some considerations on Saxo's sources, historical methods, and folk-lore by Frederick York Powell, London 1894.

[3] OLIVER ELTON. *Frederick York Powell. A life and a selection from his letters and occasional writings,* 2 vols., Oxford 1906, vol. 1 pp. 113-115.

[4] Quotations are taken from SAXONIS Gesta Danorum. Rec. et ed. J. Olrik & H. Ræder. Indicem verborum conficiendum cur. Franz Blatt, 2 vols., Copenhagen 1931-57.

[5] *Danmarks gamle Personnavne.* Udg. af Gunnar Knudsen & Marius Kristensen. Under Medvirkning af Rikard Hornby, 4 vols., København 1936-64.

[6] SNORRI STURLUSON. *Heimskringla.* Bjarni Aðalbjarnarson gaf út, 3 vols., Reykjavík 1941-51 (Íslenzk fornrit, 26-28), vol. 2 pp. 111-112 (*Óláfs saga helga,* 78).

[7] STEPHANI JOHANNIS STEPHANII *Notæ uberiores in historiam Danicam Saxonis Grammatici.* Sorø 1645. Facsimile edition with an introduction by H.D. Schepelern, Copenhagen 1978 (Danish Humanist Texts and Studies, 2).

[8] PAUL HERRMANN. *Erläuterungen zu den ersten neun Büchern der dänischen Geschichte des Saxo Grammaticus,* 2 vols. Leipzig 1901-22, vol. 1 p. 332 n.

[9] REMIGII AUTISSIODORENSIS *Commentum in Martianum Capellam.* Ed. with an introduction by Cora E. Lutz, 2 vols., Leiden 1962-65, vol. 1 pp. 188-189.

[10] RICHMOND LATTIMORE. 'Practical notes on translating Greek poetry', *On translation.* Ed. by Reuben A. Brower, Cambridge, Mass. 1959, p. 48.

THE LAY OF INGELLUS AND ITS CLASSICAL MODELS[1]

KARSTEN FRIIS-JENSEN

University of Copenhagen

As you all know Saxo inserted several longer poems and short loose stanzas into the narrative of the first part of Gesta Danorum. One of the most interesting among these poems is the longest, the so-called Lay of Ingellus.[2] It amounts to 337 lines in total, the first and larger part consisting of 280 lines in 70 sapphic stanzas and the second part of 57 hexameter lines. Formally it is a monologue in a broad sense, the words of one man. In the preceding prose narrative Saxo tells us that the old warrior Starcatherus has come to the court of king Ingellus, his foster-son. While Starcatherus was absent, the German Svertingus treacherously murdered Ingellus's father Frotho; but Ingellus has reconciled himself to Svertingus's family by marrying his daughter and receiving his sons at his sumptuous table. This state of affairs makes Starcatherus angry, and he starts his long poetic monologue, denouncing the luxury of Ingellus's court and exhorting him to avenge his father. But although we are not told what the other persons involved said, Starcatherus's monologue, so to speak, mirrors the simultaneous dramatic action caused by his words. Saxo divides the poem into three main sections by two short prose insertions, which do not interfere with the continuity of the poem. In a mixture of gnomic statements, abusive addresses to persons present in the hall, and memories of the heroic past, a strong tension is slowly built up, and as the climax of the resulting action Ingellus kills his brothers-in-law, Svertingus's sons. At this point the metre changes, and in the broad hexameter epilogue Starcatherus reflects upon Ingellus's revenge and his own life. Starcatherus's moral code is expounded throughout the poem, and the main themes are ancient Danish moderation confronted with foreign German luxury and the virtues of courage, lawful revenge, loyalty to the king, and patriotism.

The Lay of Ingellus is known solely from Gesta Danorum, but the figures of Saxo's narrative have deep roots in northern Germanic legends. In *Beowulf* (vv. 2009-2069) a scene is described in which Ingeld, a prince of the Heathobards engaged to a Danish princess, is incited by a nameless old warrior to avenge his father king Froda, who was killed by the Danes. In Norse tradition Starkaðr is well known, although he is not as complex a figure as the Starcatherus of Gesta Danorum. We even have a Norse poem about Starkaðr, the Víkarsbálkr, which is found in a *fornaldarsaga,* Gautreks saga. In this poem Starkaðr gives an account of his life, formally similar to another poem of Starcatherus in Gesta Danorum.

The most penetrating and spiritual interpretation of the Lay of Ingellus was given by Axel Olrik. His general point of view may be illustrated by the following quotation from *Danmarks Heltedigtning*[3]: "For anybody working in the vast field of popular heroic epic the Lay of Ingellus is an inexhaustible source of wonder at the high spiritual level achieved in it. The life of the individual is seen in its relationship to the cultural evolution as a whole, and the power of cultural influx on the political conditions of a country is recognized. Even more remarkable is the view of king and nation in the Lay. The king of the Bjarkamál, Rolvo, is the ideal king of his housecarls, but no people is saved by him or suffers by his fall. In our Lay the king exists for the sake of the nation. Soon a German shall occupy the throne of Lethra unless Ingellus awakens from his stupor".

But Olrik's aim was to reconstruct the vernacular poem which undoubtedly lies behind Saxo's version. Olrik thought it possible to remove all suspected additions made by Saxo and reach "the core", in his opinion a Danish alliterative poem from the middle of the tenth century. He even made a very interesting version of this poem in modern Danish, which at least bears witness to Olrik's creative artistic power. Olrik thus secured an easily accessible poetic monument for an otherwise extremely meagre period of our national literature, a period in which runic inscriptions make up the bulk. His view of the poem has been adopted by writers of Danish literary history, and his translation has found its way into anthologies of national literature.

Although I find Olrik and his followers' wish to get behind the Latin text important in principle, I distrust any result which, owing to lack of comparative material, has as its analytical starting-point a more or less subjective conception of what is ancient, nordic, and original. To me a careful analysis of Saxo's text as we have it must be the first necessary step, but secondarily this analysis might throw new light on his vernacular model.

The preconception of Saxo's Latin text as a verbose and messy paraphrase of a superior vernacular model rendered superfluous any serious considerations of Saxo's own principles of textual organization. Despite the demonstration of repetitions in thought and wording, and suggestions of radical textual omissions by Knabe, Herrmann, and Gertz, I still believe that the text of the poem can be regarded as finished by the author in accordance with a careful compositional plan. At the moment my analysis is far from being carried to its completion, but I think I have found a fruitful approach to the poem, which I shall now explain.

The language and metrical technique of the poem place it firmly in a long literary tradition, the tradition which has taken the poets of classical and late antiquity as models. This is a common feature of all Saxo's poems, but in this case it seems to be difficult to proceed further and place the poem in a well-defined genre, because the Lay by its sheer bulk exceeds the usual limits of texts in lyric metre. We certainly know that Saxo has the courage to experiment in these matters, but he usually does it in continuation of classical usage. His other poems in lyric metre are short, and one of his main sources of metrical variety, Martianus Capella, has no four-lined stanzas at all.

I have tried to obtain a general view of the classical and medieval production of poems in sapphic stanzas. Horace and Prudentius are the only ancient poets with a considerable output in this metre, Horace with 26 shorter poems, Prudentius with two hymns of 20 and 50 stanzas respectively. In the Middle Ages the sapphic stanza is the most popular of the classical lyric metres, but the poems almost never exceed twenty stanzas in length, and they are usually of a religious content. The only medieval text I have seen which in scope could be compared to Saxo is a series of nine hymns to Saint Benedict, each consisting of between 11 and 24 stanzas, 158 stanzas in total.[4] The authorship is doubtful, but the hymns have been ascribed to Alphanus of Salerno who died in 1085.[5] The Lay of Ingellus, however, is far removed from this ecclesiastic poetry, which is in the tradition of Prudentius. The longest sapphic poem I know from the period between Alphanus and Saxo consists of twenty stanzas. It is written by the monk Reginald of Canterbury[6] about 1100, and in it Reginald recommends one of his young friends to read and imitate Horace's odes, if he wants success as a poet and teacher. Both Horace and

Prudentius are likely models for Saxo's contemporaries.

Paul Herrmann is to my knowledge the only scholar who has paid any attention to this problem.[7] His reflections run as follows: Saxo found that this complaint of human viciousness was unfit for the hexameter, and chose the sapphic stanza under the influence of Prudentius's shorter hymn in this metre, *Liber cathemerinon* no. 8, "A hymn after fasting", which has some similarities of thought. Although some of Horace's odes are thematically more related to the lay than Prudentius, they are in metres different from it, and Horace is the model only for one or two phrases and a number of single words.

This makes some sense, I think. But the thematic similarities to the hymn of Prudentius are extremely weak and not corroborated by verbal loans, and the formal aspects of Prudentius' hymns are very different from anything we meet in Saxo. So my interest again focused on Horace, the model *par excellence* for Latin lyric poets. In connection with another Saxo poem, the Lay of Helga, I made Saxo's use of Horace the subject of closer examination, and I became convinced that Horace's importance had been underrated.

If Horace's odes have never been seriously taken into consideration as models for the Lay of Ingellus, one reason is the rather scanty verbal similarities mentioned. But secondly our, so to speak, spontaneous conception of Horace's odes is at variance with our view of the Lay of Ingellus, also when we regard the poem as a textual unity independent of the prose. On second thoughts, however, we must admit that Horace in his odes stands for much more than songs about drinking and pretty girls. Many of Horace's most interesting odes have satirical, moral, and political themes, just like the lay of Ingellus.

Our next problem is the formal aspect of Horace's odes: Are there any similarities between the way the *ego* of Horace's odes communicates his thoughts and that of Saxo's poem. Horace is a complex and versatile poet, difficult to square with ready formulas. Richard Heinze, one of the scholars who tried to describe the essence of Horace's odes, "das Wesen der horazischen Ode", has been blamed for being too categorical and ruthless, but for us some of his conclusions[8] are of interest, however superficial they have been considered to be: the Horatian ode is an address ("Ansprache") made by the poet to a second person, or persons. This person or persons we must imagine as present at the recitation, not as mere receivers of a written versified message. Sometimes we must even suppose a progressive action during the recitation. The poet also wants to influence the will of the person adressed, and in the verbs the imperative, the subjunctive of exhortation, and the future, are common. The attention is directed towards the future, and when the poet tells of his past it is done to provide an exemplum for his teachings. Now, all these elements are present in abundance in the Lay of Ingellus, again if we accept the *ego* of the poem as belonging to the poet Starcatherus. And Saxo does call him a poet several times and says that he has been endowed with poetic gifts by Odin. That the Lay of Ingellus in some respects fits into Heinze's definitions, is of course not enough to make the lay Horatian, but it means that that possibility is not excluded.

The real difficulty in this formal comparison, I believe, lies in the difference of length. The average length of a Horatian ode is about five or six stanzas, the maximum 20 stanzas, and although the Lay of Ingellus is easily divided into smaller parts, from three to seven according to one's taste, the poem is a unity and must be regarded as such. The only lyric Horatian text comparable in length is the sequence of the first six odes in Book III, the so-called "Roman Odes", all in alcaic stanzas. Despite the obvious difficulties connected with this comparison I feel more and more convinced that these odes constitute one of the models of the Lay, perhaps the most important next to the vernacular "original".

Before I try to demonstrate the probability of this hypothesis I shall give a short survey of the verbal parallels in Gesta Danorum to Horace's odes. Such material is in my opinion very important in establishing a relationship between two texts of this type, an a very useful corroborant when the more interesting, but perhaps also more subjective thematic similarities are discussed.

The Olrik/Ræder edition of Saxo lists only three Horatian parallels, all of them to the odes. The first is the glyconic line *regum colla potentium* (17,12), almost identical with Horace's *regum colla minacium* at ode 2,12,12. The immediate context is similar, too. The second parallel is found in Saxo's prose (144,6); twelve Norwegian brothers known for their strength have formed a gang of robbers, and Saxo describes them as among other things *iuvenes ... giganteis clari triumphis,* "young men famous for their triumphs over giants"; in Horace the words are used of Jove, ... *Iovis/clari Giganteo triumpho/,* and they are found in the first Roman Ode, at line seven. The third parallel is more elaborate. A stanza of the Lay of Ingellus is compared with a Horatian sapphic stanza:

Saxo 175,13-16
mensa perstabat modico paratu
exhibens sumptum *tenui salino,*
ne quid externo variaret usu
    docta *vetustas.*

("The table used to stand with slight display, a modest salt-cellar showing the measure of its cost, lest the wise ways of antiquity should in any way be changed by foreign usage")

Hor.carm. 2,16,13-16
vivitur parvo bene, cui *paternum*
splendet in *mensa tenui salinum*
nec levis somnos timor aut cupido
    sordidus aufert.

("He lives happily upon a little on whose frugal table gleams the ancestral salt-cellar, and whose soft slumbers are not banished by fear or sordid greed")

The words in common are *mensa, tenuis,* and *salinum* (salt-cellar, salt-dish), and instead of Horace's adjective *paternus* Saxo uses the substantive *vetustas.* The thought is the same in the two stanzas, and for both authors the modest salt-cellar is a symbol of the frugal old days. Saxo also places the borrowed words in the same position in the line as Horace.

The Swedish scholar Josef Svennung noted two other parallels to Horace in his review of the Olrik/Ræder edition[9]: The line from the Lay of Ingellus p. 177 *Daniā post te potietur heres* resembles *divitiis potietur heres* at Horace ode 2,3,20, and the resemblance is emphasized by the fact that Horace's alcaic ten-syllable line ends in the same metrical pattern as Saxo's sapphic. Svennung's other parallel is mentioned independently by Paul Herrmann,[10] too, and is the observation that two of the stanzas in the Lay of Ingellus have the same structure and subject-matter as two stanzas of Horace ode 1,22 *(Integer vitae ...),* although in other words.

I shall not go into further details, but make a preliminary conclusion: in my opinion the already established parallel material indicates that Saxo read several of Horace's odes and used them as models for both thought and wording. I must, however, make the reservation that a final careful examination of all the Horatian parallels might modify this picture. But as the material seems to grow rather than shrink at the moment, I have postponed this. Some of the Horatian loans are found in the Lay of

Ingellus, and one found in the prose of Book VI, which contains the Lay of Ingellus, shows that Saxo has read the first Roman Ode.

Now to my juxtaposition of the Roman Odes and the Lay of Ingellus. None of the verbal parallels mentioned connects these two texts directly, and some of them show that other Horatian odes have played a role for the Lay as well. I certainly do not deny this, but it is precisely in the Roman Odes that we find a very high concentration of themes also found in the Lay. One of the first problems to be faced is this: was there any possibility of Saxo's recognizing the series of six odes as a textual unity of some kind, for, as you probably know, the label "Roman Odes" is a German invention of the 19th century? I think so. There are statements by the commentator Porphyrio and the grammarian Diomedes to the effect that these six odes do constitute a unity,[11] but at the moment I know very little of how far this understanding is reflected e.g. in the annotated manuscripts of Saxo's time. Besides, Saxo is keenly interested in metrics, and he would at once realize that this sequence of several odes in the same metre is unique in Horace.

I shall now present some of my arguments in the case, proceeding from ode to ode as they are found in Horace, and noting small points and stronger evidence at the same time.

The first ode is about the blessings of a simple way of life. The rich and ambitious and their life of luxury are contrasted with people living a frugal and simple life on good terms with nature. Anxiety follows the wealthy, only the man satisfied with little is carefree, and in the end both are subject to Death. As I have said before, the prose parallel given by Olrik/Ræder comes from his ode. The solemn and prophetic tone resembles that of the Lay, and the powerful opening words *odi profanum vulgus et arceo,* "I hate the uninitiated crowd and keep them far away", are perhaps echoed in the Lay, as I shall mention later. Horace's curious picture in stanza 9, of the fish sensing their waters contracting because the rich man has decided to build his villa out into the sea, may be reflected in a rather unusual simile by Starcatherus. When being pushed down to the wall of Ingellus's hall by the extravagant king's many courtiers, he says (170,27): "Now, the lot of a nobler age is reversed; I am shut in a corner, I am like the fish that seeks shelter by flight hidden in the waters". There are other examples of animal similes in the Lay of Ingellus, but they are more traditional: Ingellus's wife feeds him like a pig

(173,17), and later on Starcatherus says that in his degrading state Ingellus can easily be murdered like a kid or a sheep (177,22ff). Ingellus's wife
is compared to a she-wolf, which will bring forth young wolves harmful to
their parent. But in these examples Starcatherus expresses a total contempt for the persons involved, whereas what he says of himself is only a
half-humorous characterization of the situation he has been brought into,
not of himself as a person.

There is, however, one longer passage where I strongly suspect the
first Roman Ode to be a model, namely the final section of the Lay, the
last 28 hexameters. This section has been condemned by Knabe and
Herrmann as being an addition of six originally unconnected fragments
left over from another stage of composition.[12] On closer inspection the
line of thought and argumentation looks very similar to that of Horace's
ode, which I think points to some sort of coherence on Saxo's part. The
Horatian contrast between luxury and ambition with anxiety on one side,
and a frugal and simple life without worries on the other side, has been
slightly altered. The simple life without worries is in the Lay the simple
life of a soldier without fear of death, also a Horatian theme, found in a
very elaborate form in the second Roman Ode. I give a translation of the
central passages, Horace first. The opening line we have heard already:
"I hate the uninitiated crowd and keep them far away". From line 9
Horace brings in several examples of rich and ambitious men: "It happens that one man lays out his vine-trees more spaciously in their furrows
than another, that this man descends to the Campus Martius a candidate
of nobler blood, that this man contends with an advantage in character
and reputation, that that man has a larger crowd of followers: with impar-
tial law Necessity (that is: Death) chooses by lot both high and low, her
capacious urn holds every name. For the man over whose impious neck a
drawn sword hangs, Sicilian feasts, though elaborate, will not produce a
pleasurable taste, the music of birds and the lyre will not bring back
sleep: gentle sleep does not despise the humble homes of country folk nor
a shady bank nor a valley fanned by west winds". And now I jump two
stanzas to the fish I mentioned before: "The fish feel their waters contract
as piles are driven down into the deep; at this point many a contractor
with his slaves, and the owner who is bored with the land, shoot down
building-rubble: but Fear and Forebodings climb as high as the owner,
and black worry does not abandon the brass-plated yacht and squats
behind the rider". Horace now concludes with a question: "But if neither

Phrygian marble nor the wearing of purple brighter than a star nor Faler-
nian wine and Persian balsam soothe a man who is troubled, why ever
should I labour to erect a hall raised high on pillars to be envied and in a
modern style? Why ever should I exchange my Sabine valley for more
troublesome riches?"

In the Lay of Ingellus Starcatherus starts by declaring that as a young
man he hated luxury, practising only war, and that he banished every
profane thing from his soul. There is a curious resemblance between
Saxo's words, *perosus* (179,26) and *mente profanum/omne relegavi*
(179,28f) and Horace's *odi profanum vulgus et arceo*. Then Starcatherus
like Horace enumerates several examples of rich, ambitious, and corrup-
ted men: "Not as with some men now, the light of whose reason is
obscured by insatiate greed with its blind maw. Some one of these dressed in an elaborate mantle effeminately guides the fleet-footed horse,
and unknots his dishevelled locks, and lets his hair fly abroad loosely. He
loves to plead often in the court, and to desire a base profit, and with this
pursuit he comforts his sluggish life, doing with venal tongue the business
entrusted to him. He outrages the laws by force, he makes armed assault
upon men's rights, he tramples on the innocent, he feeds on the wealth of
others, he practises debauchery and gluttony, he vexes good fellowship
with biting jeers, and goes after harlots as a hoe after the grass. The
coward falls when battles are lulled in peace. Though he who fears death
lie in the heart of a valley, no mantlet shall shelter him. His final fate
carries off every living man; doom is not to be averted by skulking." Like
Horace Starcatherus concludes with a question[13]: "But I, who have shaken the whole world with my slaughters, shall I enjoy a peaceful death?
Shall I be taken up to the stars in a quiet end? Shall I die in my bed
without a wound?" This comparison of Saxo and Horace raises several
interesting questions, but I must confine myself to remarking that we
perhaps now have a better understanding of the curious forensic man in
Saxo's catalogue, who has a counterpart in Horace's candidates for magi-
stracies.

The second Roman Ode is about endurance, courage, and patriotism.
The opening lines are quite in the spirit of Starcatherus: "Let the sturdy
boy learn through hard military service to suffer pinching poverty as a
friend". The central stanza of the ode reads like this: "Desirable and
glorious is a death for one's country: death follows even after the man
who runs away and does not spare the knees and timid back of a spiritless

youth". The thought is similar to that which I quoted from the final section of the Lay, and a stanza in the middle comes even closer (174,25ff): "The worthless and cowardly heart shall perish, and shall not evade the arrow of death by flight, even if it buries itself in a valley, or hides in a shady cave." That Saxo has used this stanza may also be inferred from his phrase *imbellis iuventus* in the opening line of the lay, which corresponds to Horace's *imbellis iuventa* here, and Horace's line *dulce et decorum est pro patria mori* has its parallels in other poems of Gesta Danorum, *dulce mihi, nupta, est post tua fata mori* (198,4), and *victoque metu pugnare decorum* (225,32).

The theme of Roman Ode III as expressed in the opening lines is also relevant for the Lay and for the figure of Starcatherus: "The man who is just and tenacious of his purpose neither the anger of his citizens bidding him do what is wrong nor the face of a threatening tyrant shakes from his solid determination". But the main part of the ode is occupied by Juno's long speech in the council of gods, and must have been too specifically Roman in its allusions to mythology and legend to be of any use to Saxo.

The same holds true of the fourth Roman Ode. It is an invocation of the Muses and describes the power of poetic inspiration and its political influence. There are no direct parallels to the Lay. But the power of poetic inspiration is of course relevant for the Lay, inasmuch as the Lay itself and its effect on Ingellus demonstrate this power. The fourth ode also includes a series of memories from the poet's earlier life, which serve as exempla of the main theme. Memories of Starcatherus's youth with that function are also found in abundance in the Lay.

The fifth Roman Ode also deals with martial courage and patriotism. Horace here uses two exempla from Roman history, the Roman soldiers in Parthian captivity after Crassus's defeat and the hero of the first Punic War, Regulus. There are some uncertain similarities of wording to Saxo, but in this context the first exemplum is particularly interesting. I quote the second stanza, an indignant outburst formed as a question: "Has the soldier of Crassus lived on, a husband disgraced by a barbarian wife, and – alas, the change in government and character! – has he grown old in the service of his fathers-in-law ...". The parallel to Ingellus and his marriage is obvious, and Horace's tone resembles Starcatherus's. Now we know that Ingellus's marriage is an integral part of the tradition and certainly not invented by Saxo, but similarities like this might well have directed Saxo's interest towards Horace's odes.

The sixth and last of the Roman Odes is a grave warning against moral corruption and its consequences for the state. Its final generalization is in accordance with the pessimistic Starcatherus of the sapphic part of the poem, before Ingellus's revenge. It reads: "What has destructive time not diminished? The age of our parents, worse than that of our grandparents, has produced us more wicked still, soon to give birth to a progeny yet more degenerate". Another generalizing stanza seems to have been used directly by Saxo, lines 17-20 of the ode: "Generations prolific in sin first polluted marriage and the family and home; ruin, channelled from this source, flowed out over country and people", *hoc fonte derivata clades/in patriam populumque fluxit*. A simile of the same sort is used of Ingellus (177,5-8): "Even as in a ship all things foul gather to the filthy hollow of the bilge, even so has a flood of vices poured into Ingellus", the wording *sic in Ingellum vitiosa rerum/copia fluxit* resembling Horace's *clades/in patriam populumque fluxit*. The connection between Saxo and Horace in this place is strengthened, I think, by a phrase in the prose section preceding the Lay. – Here I must insert the remark that in some respects this prose section has the form of a summary of the Lay, and it is of a certain interest because in it Saxo so to speak interprets his own poem; but time does not allow me to deal with this aspect. – However, in the prose we find a similar phrase to the effect that luxury has flowed from Germany out over our country, *in patriæ nostræ fauces ... fluxerunt* (167,27f.)

Before I begin to conclude I must explain why the title of the paper mentions the classical 'models', in the plural, of the Lay. One of Horace's satires, the second of Book II, is the chief model of the gastronomic details of the Lay, and of course Valerius Maximus with his chapters *De luxuria et libidine* (9,1) and *De institutis antiquis* (2,1-6) among others plays an important ideological role. But my experience up till now is that Valerius Maximus is a complementary source for Saxo, not a competitor to Horace, and so I have found it justifiable to concentrate on the odes.

Now back to the Roman Odes. If my arguments are convincing, the whole thing has considerable importance, I think, for our understanding of Saxo as a writer. But I do not feel that all the pieces of this jig-saw puzzle have found their place yet, so that the following is of a very preliminary character.

Firstly Saxo must have been a competent reader of Horace. We know that there existed a corpus of scholia, explanatory notes, on Horace, most of them sensible. But we know very little of the way Horace's odes were read, and of the actual use of these scholia in the Middle Ages. This Saxo can illuminate. Although he need not have understood every single allusion to contemporary Rome, he must have known the outlines of the political situation, Augustus's reforms and Horace's support of this policy. These issues are of importance as the background of the Roman Odes, and the scholia give some information. But he has also been able to extract the general, and to actualize it by drawing parallels to his own time and to the raw material he wanted to adapt. The most prominent feature of his adaption is the moral code which emerges, no doubt a synthesis of his personal view, Horace's, and that of the vernacular model of the Lay. But the corresponding evolutionary concept, which is a manifest example of cultural pessimism, has a very strong Roman flavour. As far as I know it is not found in Norse tradition in this form, but it is very common in Roman literature. It is a glorification of the moral standards in primitive societies, either barbarian nations of the far north, or the Roman nation itself at an early stage of its history, before it became hellenized, as in the Roman Odes[14]. Different pairs of contrasting words then are in existence: e.g. Greek versus Roman, contemporary Roman versus ancient Roman. Perhaps under influence of the model where the primitive society glorified is of the far north, Saxo identifies Roman with Danish, Greek with German, and ancient Roman with ancient Danish.

This conception of Saxo as a creative writer is not new, but the poet Saxo has until now been overshadowed by the prose writer. In his analysis of the Lay of Ingellus Olrik pointed out some important features, but his analytical approach now seems more problematic. The "high spiritual level achieved" and the concepts of cultural evolution and influx of a foreign culture in the poem do not necessarily come from the vernacular "original", but can just as well be a result of the poet Saxo's Horatian studies. But what Danish literature of the tenth century might have lost is regained two hundred years later. The Lay of Ingellus can be regarded as a genuine product of the late twelfth century, rising from a fruitful combination of Nordic and Latin tradition. This makes it more attractive to attempt an interpretation which places the poem in a late twelfth-century political and cultural context. This interpretation must be founded in a careful compositional analysis, a laborious task for so extensive a text. But some results can be expected from this attempt, since the actuality of Saxo's political and moral message was no doubt his strongest motivation for this creative work. Another aspect of his message is its function as cultural propaganda for Denmark in a Europe united by Latin culture. I believe that the figure of Starcatherus has a specific role in this propaganda. An earlier examination[15] of another poem of Starcatherus, the Lay of Helga, brought the rather surprising result that the poem is a conscious imitation of a Roman satire, in the vein of Horace and Juvenal. The Starcatherus of Gesta Danorum is perhaps then Saxo's attempt at creating a classical Danish poet comparable to the great Roman models and with the technical skill of a Horace. Consequently Saxo's story of Starcatherus can be considered a sort of scald's saga in Latin.

[1] This paper on the Lay of Ingellus presents some preliminary results obtained in a general investigation, still in progress, of the poetry of Gesta Danorum. My methodical approach to verbal loans from the classics is expounded in a critical survey of Saxo's alleged Virgilian parallels: *Saxo og Vergil. En analyse af 1931-udgavens Vergilparalleller*, København 1975 (Opuscula Graecolatina, 1). The translations of Saxo and Horace in the paper are mostly Oliver Elton's and Gordon William's (from *The third book of Horace's Odes*. Edited with translation and running commentary by Gordon Williams, © Oxford University Press 1969; by permission of Oxford University Press).

[2] The Lay of Ingellus is found at the end of Book VI, pp. 170,11-180,13 in Olrik/Ræder's edition, which is also used at all other references to Gesta Danorum.

[3] AXEL OLRIK. *Danmarks Heltedigtning*, vol. 2. p. 42, København 1910. The translation is mine.

[4] Printed in ARNOLDUS WION. *Lignum vitae, ornamentum et decus Ecclesiae*, lib. 3, pp. 85-101, Venezia 1595.

[5] See MAX MANITIUS. *Geschichte der lateinischen Literatur des Mittelalters*, vol. 2. p. 636f., München 1923 (Handbuch der Altertums-Wissenschaft IX,2).

[6] Best edition in JACOB HAMMER. 'A monastic panegyrist of Horace', *Philological Quarterly* vol. 11 (1932) pp. 303-310.

[7] PAUL HERRMANN. *Erläuterungen zu den ersten neun Büchern der dänischen Geschichte des Saxo Grammaticus*, vol. 2 p. 464, Leipzig 1922.

[8] 'Die horazische Ode' (1923), reprinted in RICHARD HEINZE. *Vom Geist des Römertums*. Hrsg. von Erich Burck, 3. erw. Aufl., pp. 172-189, Darmstadt 1960.

[9] JOSEF SVENNUNG's review of the Olrik/Ræder edition appeared in *Arkiv för nordisk filologi* vol. 55 (1940) p. 122ff.

[10] HERRMANN op.cit. p. 464.

[11] Mentioned, among others, by RICHARD HEINZE. 'Der Zyklus der Römeroden' (1929), p. 192 in *Vom Geist des Römertums* ... (see above note 8). The passages are PORPHYRIO ad Hor.carm. 3,1,1 and DIOMEDES ars gramm. lib. 3, p. 525,1-6 Keil.

[12] HERRMANN op.cit. p. 464. Cf. the critical apparatus of Olrik/Ræder's edition to 179,25.

[13] Olrik/Ræder without sufficient reason changed the question-mark of the editio princeps into a full stop. Cf. SVENNUNG op.cit. p. 122.

[14] See EDUARD FRAENKEL. *Horace*, p. 241, Oxford 1957.

[15] Still unpublished. Cf. above note 1.

THE ICELANDIC SOURCES OF SAXO GRAMMATICUS

BJARNI GUÐNASON

University of Iceland

Foreign learning and a native cultural heritage are combined in so unique a manner in *Gesta Danorum* that Saxo's monumental work has neither prototype nor imitation in the literature of Scandinavia. Research on Saxo has suffered on this account, since for a long time scholars have neglected to place his writings in a wider cultural context. In recent years, however, there have been progressive attempts to explain and understand Gesta Danorum in terms of continental Catholic culture, and these have produced some fruitful results.

But in dealing with Saxo's actual sources the same comprehensiveness of approach has not always been in evidence, and it seems to me that there is a real need for their examination from the viewpoint of the Nordic cultural area as a whole.

Such an approach leads one to the literature of medieval Iceland, which, both for quantity and quality, is bound to provide a basis for researches into the literary culture of the northern countries. The Icelanders composed a few sagas about kings of the earliest Danish dynasties, the Skjǫldungar and Knýtlingar, using both oral and written sources.[1] No adequate research on these sagas can be carried out without reference to Danish sources, and above all Saxo. And naturally the same applies to Saxo himself. The scholar who tries to tackle his sources while ignoring Icelandic narratives is not doing justice to his task.

The researches which I have carried out on the stories of the Danish kings indicate that there is a closer connexion between Icelandic narratives and Saxo's work than has been generally recognized. This opinion is not only the product of an Icelandic viewpoint, but also of a recognition that the deeply-rooted romantic attitude which postulated isolation as a main condition of medieval Icelandic literature has proved illusory and misleading.

Iceland was not only a storehouse of ancient traditions. Thanks to close links with other nations it was also the scene of unremitting literary creativity. The literature itself provides ample proof that, in spite of geographical isolation, those cultural links with other nations were close. Admittedly the Icelanders were receivers. They sought learning far and wide, in foreign schools, taking home with them stories, books, and knowledge. But they were also givers.

Communication between the institutions of the Church in the northern countries was less restricted than is generally supposed. The archiepiscopal sees at Lund and Nidaros, the episcopal sees, and the monasteries were by no means cultural desert islands. At the beginning of historical records Lund was not only the metropolitan see of the Danes, but for half a century (1104-1153) of the Norwegians and Icelanders also, and seven Icelandic bishops were consecrated there.

The court scalds may be regarded as representatives of a cultural heritage with its roots in Scandinavian heathendom, but it would not be right to make too much of the difference between them and the twelfth-century Icelandic bishops, most of whom, in spite of their clerical education, were members of distinguished families whose part in preserving and developing the ancient national heritage was no small one.

Saxo mentions Arnoldus Tylensis, a member of the suite of Archbishop Absalon, of whom he says that he was learned in ancient sagas and told them well.[2] This Arnaldr is named in *Skáldatal*,[3] an ancient roll of Icelandic court poets, where he is said to be the scald of Valdemar the Great. Other poets of twelfth- and thirteenth-century Danish kings are mentioned in the list.

Although Saxo's reference to Arnaldr is a brief one, it gives a fair idea of the position and function of Icelandic scalds and agrees with several references in Icelandic writings. These poets were professionals who not only composed court verses, but also entertained with narratives in both verse and prose. Kings and chieftains were eager to hear of the heroic exploits of their forbears. One scald learned from another. It this way the traditions, training in narrative art, and conformity to Nordic culture were all assured.

The literature of Iceland came into being in the early part of the twelfth century, and must have enhanced the reputation of the Icelanders as authorities on ancient times, so that when the recording of history began in Denmark and Norway later in the same century, there was a demand for their historical learning, whether oral or in writing. The contemporaries Sven Aggesen, Saxo, and the Norwegian Theodoricus all refer to the Icelanders in the introductions to their books, so that it is self-evident that these historians made a special point of providing themselves with written sources from Icelanders, whether genealogies, chronicles, sagas of saints, or sagas of kings. And by about the year 1200 writings of this description were by no means scarce. This applies especially to Saxo, who spent between thirty and forty years compiling his history, according to estimates, so that I have little doubt that he had access to most of the Icelandic works that touched on the history of the Danes. What he took from these, and how he treated it, is another matter.

Cultural reciprocity is a basic factor in explaining the literary achievements of the Nordic cultural area.

In his Preface Saxo says:

> Nec Tylensium industria silentio oblitteranda: qui cum ob nativam soli sterilitatem luxuriæ nutrimentis carentes officia continuæ sobrietatis exerceant omniaque vitæ momenta ad excolendam alienorum operum notitiam conferre soleant, inopiam ingenio pensant. Cunctarum quippe nationum res gestas cognosse memoriæque mandare voluptatis loco reputant, non minoris gloriæ iudicantes alienas virtutes disserere quam proprias exhibere. Quorum thesauros historicarum rerum pignoribus refertos curiosius consulens, haud parvam præsentis operis partem ex eorum relationis imitatione contexui, nec arbitros habere contempsi, quos tanta vetustatis peritia callere cognovi.[4]

To the best of my knowledge, no medieval historian has ever used such glowing words of the part played by literature in the life of a poor nation as Saxo does about the Icelanders.

He remarks, for example, that they spend all the hours of their lives in acquiring knowledge of the deeds of others, and that their pleasure is to know of the achievements of other nations and to relate them. He declares that he has made a diligent search among the treasures of their history and that no small part of his work is founded on their narratives.

This Preface has not unnaturally induced scholars to speculate on the Icelanders' part in Saxo's work, but in so doing they have directed their attention almost exclusively to Saxo's legendary history (Books 1-9).

It is clear to scholars nowadays that, both in form and substance, Saxo's Preface is modelled on medieval conventions relating to such works and is therefore no reliable basis for an overall explanation of the origins of Gesta Danorum and Saxo's sources. And since the scalds and saga-writers of Iceland were highly esteemed for their historical learning, Saxo's remarks might be considered no more than a stylistic embellishment and not to be taken literally.

For this reason some have attached more weight to other evidence which they claim to find in Saxo's text itself, and little to his Preface. K. Hald, who believed *Brávallakvæði (-þula)* to be Norwegian, remarks in one place: "... det sikre er, at Saxo utvivlsomt bevidst vildleder læserne med sine oplysninger både i fortalen og her i indledningen til Bråvalla-kvadet".[5] K. Hald refers here to the Icelanders' contribution to Saxo's work. But the words are there, and the burden of proof lies on those who would discount the truth of Saxo's statement, and not on those who would take his words literally. And the fact is that I have found no valid evidence to falsify Saxo's assertion. On the contrary, most of it points the other way. This is not to say that the whole truth is thereby told. Saxo's words are so general that it cannot be deduced from them with any certainty, for example, whether the Icelandic sources used by him were oral or written ones. However, it must be remembered that no clear-cut distinction between oral and written sources existed in the minds of men at the beginning of historical writing.

In spite of the bonus unquestionably offered us by the introductory words of Saxo, the opinions of scholars on the subject have been very divided. Right up to the end of the last century nearly all Danish scholars assumed that Saxo drew almost exclusively on Danish narrative sources. This view is out of date, thanks especially to A. Olrik, whose key work *Kilderne til Sakses oldhistorie* groups the legendary history of Saxo in two classes, according to its sources in Danish or Norse (i.e. Norwegian-Icelandic) narratives. This division is still largely accepted.

But Olrik's theory has been criticized, among other reasons for his assertion that the "Norse" narratives used by Saxo were in fact Norwegian, whereas some scholars, especially German[6] (and needless to say Icelandic!) ones, think that he used Icelandic rather than Norwegian narratives. Since there are scholars who still hold firmly to Olrik's view, I feel obliged to make a few general observations about it. But I shall draw no veil over the fact that this is *a priori* by no means an easy matter to settle, since the Norwegians and Icelanders spoke the same language and had close cultural ties.

The first point to consider is that Olrik had Icelandic legendary sagas to support his researches, for no Norwegian sagas of this kind have survived and little is known of them. Olrik evidently intends to credit the words of the Preface by supposing that Saxo's informant was an Icelander (i.e. Arnoldus Tylensis). However, his argument for Saxo having only one informant is not convincing. Moreover, this compromise is itself an embarrassment, for with an Icelandic informant or informants it would unquestionably have been more reasonable to suppose that Saxo's Norse narratives were not only Norwegian but also Icelandic.

Olrik's main argument was that, where comparison could be made, the divergences between the Icelandic sources and Saxo were too great for the latter to have used them. But here it is important to bear in mind both what kind of literary genre the legendary sagas are, and no less what method of work Saxo adopted.

The legendary sagas are stories designed to entertain, telling of heroes and vikings, and of events that took place, especially in Scandinavia, before Iceland was settled. Olrik's theory of an Icelandic informant, but Norwegian narratives, is based on the assumption that the stories had acquired a fixed form and that the Icelanders had played no part in their creation or formation. This is hard to accept. We have positive examples of named storytellers and scalds who entertained gatherings in Iceland in the earlier part of the twelfth century by themselves composing "legendary sagas", basing them on old traditions, story-motives, and *märchen,* and making poems and verses for them.

In C.C. Rafn's edition of 1829-30 there are about thirty Icelandic "legendary sagas", many of which had existed in more than one version. For example, it appears that there were three or four versions about each of the two Skjǫldungar, Hrólfr kraki and Ragnarr loðbrók, and these versions differed in content, order of events, and characters. It may be mentioned that the *Skjǫldunga Saga* narrative about Hrólfr kraki and Vǫggr is influenced by the *Dialogues of Gregorius,* translated into Icelandic in the twelfth century, while the complete surviving version of *Hrólfs Saga* is influenced by sagas of chivalry of the thirteenth century. New tastes, new tales.

These sagas were episodic in content, especially when dealing with vikings who went on unorganized raids from one country to another. An extra raid could always be added, or another story-motive. Traditional tales were repeatedly imitated. Motives were extracted from them and put into new contexts. Ancient events were linked with new characters and old heroes played a part in new adventures. An endless interchange of story-material took place.

Nobody questions the existence of oral verses and tales about legendary heroes and vikings in Norway, as elsewhere in the viking settlements of Scandinavia, which were later brought in some form to Iceland, beside stories and migrant themes from distant lands.

It may well be that Hrólfr kraki and King Aðils of Uppsala were originally kings of the Heruli and of the Huns in the fourth and fifth centuries, and that some story-motifs about Ragnarr loðbrók derived from Flanders as N. Lukman has maintained.[7] But in spite of all this Saxo's narratives may be Icelandic, in the same way as the later Eddic poems dealing with Sigurðr Fáfnisbani, to say nothing of *Grípisspá* and *Sigurðarkviða in skamma,* were in all likelihood composed in Iceland. Here a clear distinction has to be made between the provenance of saga-elements and story-motifs, and the saga-form om which Saxo based his work. It may be assumed that the Icelandic contribution consisted especially in the organization of heterogeneous and fragmentary story-material into a greater unity, fashioning complete sagas in conformity with a system.

A. Olrik called the Norwegian narratives "skippersagaer," whose native habitat was the west coast of Norway, but it would be difficult to find evidence to show that these alleged sagas had reached the stage of development to which Saxo and the Icelandic sagas bear witness.

Let us turn now to Saxo's method of work. Since the researches of C. Weibull[8] scholars have acquired a new understanding of this, and Olrik's conclusions might have been different had he been fully aware of its character. Saxo puts his stories and story-themes into new contexts, reverses and changes, mixes unrelated material, and spices his narrative with anecdotes and elucidations. He is the patriot and the cleric who gives his material a new overall interpretation conforming to the moral message of the heroic age and the system of virtues and vices of the Church. Saxo's Latin style and elaboration of language also differentiate his narrative widely from that of his sources. In other words, Saxo renders his sources almost unrecognizable.

Yet, in spite of the character of legendary sagas, and of Saxo's methods, the relationship between his work and the Icelandic legendary sagas is in many cases quite obvious, as Olrik has shown better than any other. The conclusion should therefore be clear. But modern scholars are reluctant to speak of links between narratives unless certain conditions are fulfilled. And if a literary relationship is to be asumed, the conditions are severe: the story-material must correspond in detail, the sequence of events be similar, and last but not least, there must be verbal similarities to clinch the matter. Saxo seldom fulfils all these conditions simultaneously, so that it is not really surprising that there should have been some difficulty in reaching conclusions regarding his sources, especially where oral ones are involved.

Both Saxo and Icelandic authorities indicate that there was an abundance of material in existence about Starkaðr. I shall not make too little of the differences, but in many places the relationship is so close that some scholars would go much farther than A. Olrik, concluding that Saxo's sources on Starkaðr were largely Icelandic, both verse and prose (A. Heusler and others). One of the poems which is put into the mouth of Starkaðr is *Brávallaþula,* and since it has been very much in the limelight in discussions on Saxo's Norse authorities, I have a few words to say about it.

Brávallaþula is found in prose form in Saxo's eighth book and also in an Icelandic manuscript from about 1300, known as *Sǫgubrot af fornkonungum,* or fragments from ancient kings.[9] It is a roll of the champions who took part in the battle at Brávellir, and behind it there lies an old poem, probably composed in the *fornyrðislag* metre.

A great deal has been written about this poem, and sometimes with the most extraordinary conclusions.[10] For instance, S. Bugge believed that the *þula* was composed between 6 and 10 September 1066, while Harald Hardrada, king of Norway, was sailing along the coast of Scotland on his way to Northumberland.[11] This dating still has a following. Olrik, on the other hand, considered the *þula* to be undoubtedly Norwegian, but composed in Telemark, in view of the praise of the people of that region found in it.[12] And there is more of the same kind.

Olrik made much of the fact that the Norse legendary sagas of Saxo contained Norwegian place-names, and concluded that they were therefore Norwegian. However, this argument can hardly stand, for it could be used to prove that not a single one of the legendary sagas in Icelandic literature was Icelandic. Since these stories all take place in a period

before Iceland was settled, they are bound to deal with Norwegians and
events in Norway, among other matters, and to mention Norwegian place-names. Olrik's argument could equally well be used to prove that
Heimskringla was Norwegian. And then he reverses it to maintain that
since Saxo mentions Icelanders (and Icelandic place-names) in his account of the battle at Brávellir, the *þula* cannot be Icelandic, for no
Icelander would have made his fellow-countrymen take part in a battle in
legendary times. But those who are familiar with Icelandic literature will
not be able to accept this argument. The *þula* was composed to entertain.
Its author brings all the principal champions of Europe together to a
battle in one place. He knows perfectly well that Starkaðr, Bjarki, the
vikings of Jómsborg, and the rest never fought at Brávellir. He knows
that Starkaðr and Ubbi, the main heroes of his creation, never met in
single combat, nor did Starkaðr kill Ella, the antagonist of Ragnar loðbrók. Norwegians fight Norwegians, Icelanders with Icelanders, and so
on. The poet lets his imagination run away with him in his comedy, caring
neither for time nor place.

Needless to say, scholars have examined the personal names and their
morphology in Saxo's roll of champions. D.A. Seip made a special contribution in this field, and in the main his conclusions are accepted.[13] He
believed that the *þula* was Norwegian, in all probability recorded at
Tunsberg, from where it came into Saxo's hands. In other words, the
personal names showed marks of south-eastern Norwegian linguistic features. But Seip fails to take into account the state of the manuscripts of
Gesta Danorum, especially where the roll of champions is concerned, nor
does he ever answer the question whether the condition of the text itself
will allow an unambiguous conclusion to be drawn about the place of
origin of the *þula* from the personal names in it. The answer, of course,
must be no. There is such confusion in the name-endings, both in the
Paris version of 1514 and the Danish translation of Kristiern Pedersen,
that it is extremely doubtful whether anything can be said one way or
another about the provenance of the *þula* from them. Besides which, it is
bound to be a very uncertain foundation for any scholarly conclusions, if
these are based on the orthography of a very few word-forms and endings, when Saxo's roll contains some 250 names (165 names of champions and 47 nicknames, beside patronymics and place-names).

It should also be mentioned that Seip's attempt to prove the south-
eastern Norwegian origins of the *þula* with reference to an *a*-glide before

r in the endings does not succeed (Dagr>Dahar, Sámr>Sambar; and in Sǫgubrot: Krókr>Krókarr). Norwegian linguistic remains do not warrant such a conclusion.

Saxo declares that Starkaðr composed a poem which was in the Danish tongue and lived on the lips of the common people without being written down. The *þula* is also put into the mouth of Starkaðr in Icelandic authorities, while the Danish tongue can mean the language spoken throughout the Scandinavian lands. Saxo's assertion can therefore stand, and the distorted words, corruptions, and confusion in endings may well be explained by Saxo having either written down the poem, or had it written, and the accumulation of errors occurring as the text was copied and printed.

It is noteworthy that Seip remarks that his conclusions provide no solution to the problem of explaining Saxo's mention of Icelandic place-names. Saxo mentions both Icelanders and Icelandic place-names. He refers to the districts of Skagafjörður, Miðfjörður, and Brynjudalur, and to the farm Sker. In the *Sǫgubrot* these names are wanting, and the most likely explanation of this is that, as said before, the *þula* was originally intended for entertainment only, but when written down much later it had become historical, and hence these family features disappeared.[14]

Of course no conclusive proof of the Icelandic provenance of *Brávallaþula* can be afforded by these arguments, the state of the text being what it is. However, if it were possible to show literary connexions between Saxo and the Icelandic authorities, this would be bound to weigh considerably in all these discussions on the Norwegian or Icelandic sources of his work. Where Saxo's legendary material is concerned, there are two authorities in particular to be considered: *the genealogy of the men of Oddi and the Skjǫldungar,* and *Skjǫldunga Saga.*

Sven Aggesen explains how the Danish kings derive their name from Skjǫldr and are called Skjǫldungar in Icelandic poems "A quo primum modis Hislandensibus Skioldunger sunt reges <nostri> nuncupati."[15]

One of the most powerful clans in Iceland in the twelfth and thirteenth centuries was that of the Oddverjar, or men of Oddi, who regarded themselves as the descendants of the Skjǫldungar, the ancient Danish kings. They compiled the roll of their lineage at a very early date, and it has survived to this day. There is a strong possibility that its author was Sæmundr the Learned (d. 1133).

There are various reasons for believing that Sven Aggesen had access to the Oddverjar lineage, among them the fact that he does not agree with the *Chronicon Lethrense*[16] of 1170 in naming Dan as the ancestor of the Danish kings, but names Skjǫldr, and has moreover eight generations in virtually the same order, with the single exception of Uffa, whom he puts in the place of Olaf the Humble.

Saxo's roll of kings is completely chaotic, with about 60 kings in a confusion of names drawn from various story-cycles; but it has some obviously Danish features, with Dan first, and so on. In one place Saxo remarks, "Hic (i.e. Uffo) a compluribus Olavus est dictus atque ob animi moderationem Mansueti cognomine donatus".[17] As Olrik has pointed out,[18] this must come from Icelandic sources, since Sven Aggesen makes no reference to Olaf the Humble, as already indicated.

Icelandic influence on Saxo's roll of kings came by two channels: on the one hand from Sven, and on the other direct from an Icelandic genealogy. This may have stood on its own, or Sven and Saxo may each have found it in Skjǫldunga Saga itself, or perhaps both. Time will not allow an explanation of the origins of the genealogy, but I shall just mention that its compiler chiefly used names which he obtained from oral tradition and found in poems about the Skjǫldungar, and that the number of generations was 27, as in the ancient poem *Ynglingatal*.[19]

Skjǫldunga Saga was compiled about the year 1200 and tells of all the kings from Skjǫldr, son of Odin (an influence from English dynastic tables), to Gormr the Old. Only disconnected fragments of it have survived. The ancient genealogy of the Skjǫldungar and Oddverjar provided its basis, while the author was also familiar with a substantial body of sagas and poems about the Skjǫldungar (like the author of the genealogy), though he follows the genealogy closely and allows himself little in the way of digression (principally about Hrólfr kraki and Ragnarr loðbrók). The saga has a learned flavour and is, in intention, a saga of kings rather than a legendary saga, as its theme might suggest.

There are some indications that Skjǫldunga Saga was used by Saxo; and attention has been drawn in particular to the statement in it that the Peace of Fróði was in the days of the Emperor Augustus, when Christ was born into the world.

Saxo has the same dating for the Peace of Fróði, and this is unknown elsewhere.[20] It may be added that there are some passages in both the Saga and Saxo which are obviously closely related, but of this I shall say no more here.

It is worth noting that Bishop Páll Jónsson of Skálholt was consecrated by Archbishop Absalon in 1195. Páll had been studying in England, probably at Lincoln, but was a layman and a secular chieftain at the time when he went to receive consecration. Bishop Páll was directly descended from Sæmundr the Learned on the male side. Some have surmised that Páll himself was the author of Skjǫldunga Saga.[21]

In researches into the Icelandic sources of Saxo, no serious investigations have been considered worth making on whether he might have used Icelandic accounts in the historical portions of his work (Books 10-16), although Icelandic sagas touching on the subjects of his narrative had been compiled by the year 1200. However, there is one exception to this: Inge Skovgaard-Petersen has in an excellent article[22] argued that Saxo's accounts of Harald Bluetooth and Svein Forkbeard show probable familiarity with twelfth-century Icelandic historical works. The works in question are *Jómsvíkinga Saga* and the *Saga of Óláfr Tryggvason* of the monk Oddr Snorrason. I have myself pointed out two other twelfth-century written authorities, a poem and a saga, which I believe Saxo used in his historical portion.

In *Knýtlinga Saga,* a work from the mid-thirteenth century, there is an obituary poem on Eiríkr eigóði, King of the Danes (d. 1103).[23] It is called *Eiríksdrápa,* and it lists the principal events of his life: his journeys to Russia and to Rome, his campaign against the Wends, the foundation of the archiepiscopal see at Lund, his journey to Jerusalem, and so on. The author of the poem was the Icelandic lawspeaker Markús Skeggjason (d. 1107).

Needless to say, Saxo gives an account of Eiríkr eigóði and gets his material from earlier written sources which will not be dealt with here. However, it appears to me that the relationship between Eiríksdrápa and Saxo is quite unequivocal.[24] Although comparisons between Saxo and Icelandic court poetry inevitably tend to produce somewhat uncertain conclusions, that he made direct use of Eiríksdrápa, including elements of it in his text with his customary circumlocutions, is a matter of virtual certainty. Scholars have pointed out Saxo's failure to understand the ancient scaldic language, and Eiríksdrápa is a case in point. Saxo failed to understand the kenning *brynþings beiðir* (i.e. warrior), and it is quite instructive to see how his misunderstanding was the occasion of a new story. The creator is caught in the act.[25].

Jón Qgmundarson was the first Icelandic bishop to be consecrated by Archbishop Qzurr at Lund, on 19 April 1106. It is more than likely that Bishop Jón had the *drápa* of Markús the Lawspeaker with him and recited it to the Danish king Nikolas, brother of Eiríkr eigóði, in the presence of the archbishop, who is highly praised in it. The poem mentions the foundation of the arch-see, which was probably the true occasion of its composition.

Verbal similarities show that Saxo had access to the *drápa* in written form. He may have found this fine poem in the library at Lund, or obtained it from his Icelandic informant.

In his Heimskringla Snorri Sturluson quotes the work by the Icelander Eiríkr Oddsson known as *Hryggjarstykki*. In all probability it gave an account of three years (1136-39) in the history of Norway, and its central character was Sigurðr slembidjákn, who believed himself to be of royal birth, a son of King Magnús Barefoot (d. 1103). He attempted to win the crown of Norway by force, killing the king, Haraldr gilli in 1136, but was himself defeated three years later by the sons of Haraldr in a battle off the coast of Bóhúslén. Being captured, he was put to death with terrible tortures, and it may be surmised that the work was composed to support the cause of his canonization. It dates from about 1150, and was probably the first of its kind to be written in Iceland in the vernacular. I should mention that Sigurðr had spent one winter in Iceland.

There is an account of Sigurðr in Saxo's fourteenth Book[26]. Two features of this draw one's attention. In the first place the account is incorporated into a history of Valdimarr Knútsson describing events that happened nearly thirty years after the death of Sigurðr. And in the second place the relationship to Icelandic accounts is quite obvious.

The Danes were allies of Sigurðr. Of the thirty ships with him in the final battle, eighteen were Danish. The Danes later fetched the body of Sigurðr and had it buried at the Mariukirkja in Aalborg. And finally, one of Eiríkr Oddsson's informants was the provost Ketill (d. 1150), later canonized.

Saxo devotes so much detail to Sigurðr because he was moved by his heroism. He died a martyr, and according to Saxo his death was a pattern for the servants of the Church to follow.

All Saxo's main details about Sigurðr are also found in Heimskringla. Admittedly there are some minor discrepancies, which to my mind are the product of Saxo's method and his interpretation, though they have sufficed to make scholars in general assume that he relied on oral traditions, and probably Norwegian ones. Saxo's view of Sigurðr is the same as that of the Icelanders. In the account of his defence on board ship, his capture, and his torture there are thirteen minor details all in virtually identical order. Finally the verbal similarities are conclusive. The most obvious explanation is that Saxo made direct use of Hryggjarstykki.[27]

I believe that I have now been able to establish finally that a positive connexion existed between Saxo and Icelandic historical writing in the twelfth century. If this is correct, then the overall picture is clarified.

The conclusion of these enquiries, then, is that Saxo used oral and written Icelandic sources, and in both the legendary and historical portions of Gesta Danorum. But it should be metioned as well that the Icelanders made use of Danish historical works, too. In Knýtlinga Saga there is reference to "learned Danish books"[28], by which was probably meant annals, Ælnoth's life of St. Knut, and Saxo.[29] It bears eloquent witness to the reciprocal nature of literary influences in the Nordic cultural area.

An Icelandic contribution to Saxo's work being established, the question arises, how great was it?

When A. Olrik divided Saxo's legendary stories into two groups according to sources, the Norse (or Norwegian and Icelandic) group formed no small part. But it seems to me that his division is not complete by his own criteria, for he is somewhat over-generous to the Danish group. I am thinking here of the stories of Starkaðr, Hrólfr kraki, and Ragnarr loðbrók, for example. However, in view of Saxo's methods, it is clearly not practicable to draw an accurate distinction between Danish and Icelandic (or Norse) sources.

In the last resort it cannot be conceded that Saxo intended to mislead his readers by his introductory remarks about the contribution of Icelanders. His words: "Quorum thesauros historicarum rerum pignoribus refertos curiosius consulens, haud parvam præsentis operis partem ex eorum relationis imitatione contexui ..." seem to demand to be taken literally.

I shall say nothing about the effect this conclusion may have on enquiries into internal features of Gesta Danorum, such as the concept of the heroic, the creation of character, and the structure. But one thing is certain, and that is that the origins of the work will be made much more intelligible by the elimination of mysterious so-called "skippersagaer" of

Norwegian origin, and by seeking explanations in the wealth of sagas, the saga-entertainment, and the saga-writing of Icelanders in the twelfth century.

[1] i.e. *Skjǫldunga saga, Jómsvíkinga saga, Knýtlinga saga, Ragnars saga loðbrókar* and *Hrólfs saga kraka*.

[2] SAXONIS *Gesta Danorum*. Rec. et ed. J. Olrik & H. Ræder, vol. 1, Copenhagen 1931, pp. 459,34-460,7. AXEL OLRIK. 'Arnald Islænding', *Nordisk tidskrift för vetenskap, konst och industri* 1911 pp. 250-262.

[3] *Skáldatal* is edited in *Edda Snorra Sturlusonar*, vol. 3, Copenhagen 1880-87, pp. 251-286.

[4] GD 5,1-9.

[5] KRISTIAN HALD. 'Navnestoffet hos Saxo', *Saxostudier*. Red. Ivan Boserup, København 1975 (Opuscula Graecolatina, 2), p. 90.

[6] HERMANN SCHNEIDER. *Germanische Heldensage*, vol. II,1 (Berlin & Leipzig 1933), p. 14. – ANDREAS HEUSLER. 'Zur Skiöldungendichtung', *Zeitschrift für deutsches Altertum*, vol. 48 (1906) p. 57. – PAUL HERRMANN. *Erläuterungen zu den ersten neun Büchern der dänischen Geschichte des Saxo Grammaticus*, vol. 2, Leipzig 1922, p. 13ff. – GUSTAV NECKEL. 'Saxo Grammaticus', *Hoops' Reallexikon der germanischen Altertumskunde*, vol. 4, Strassburg 1918-19, p. 87.

[7] NIELS LUKMAN, *Skjoldunge und Skilfinge*, Copenhagen 1943. – id., 'Ragnarr loðbrók, Sigifrid, and the Saints of Flanders', *Mediaeval Scandinavia*, vol. 9 (1976) pp. 7-50.

[8] CURT WEIBULL. *Saxo*, Lund 1915. – id., 'Saxo-studier', *Historisk tidskrift för Skåneland*, vol. 7 (1917-21), pp. 71-120.

[9] Published in *Sǫgur Danakonunga*. Udg. af Carl af Petersens og Emil Olson, København 1919-25.

[10] See BJARNI GUÐNASON. 'Um Brávallaþulu', *Skírnir*, vol. 132 (Reykjavík 1958) pp. 82-128 and lit. cited there; also *Kulturhistorisk leksikon for nordisk middelalder* s.v. (D.A. SEIP).

[11] SOPHUS BUGGE. *Norsk sagafortælling og sagaskrivning i Irland*, Kristiania 1901-08, pp. 78-164 (esp. 109-113).

[12] AXEL OLRIK. 'Bråvallakvadets kæmperække' *Arkiv för nordisk filologi*, vol. 10 (1894) pp. 223-287. He discusses the poem in some other works of his (cf. *Kulturhistorisk leksikon...*).

[13] D.A. SEIP. 'Det norske grunnlag for Bråvallakvadet hos Saxo', *Norsk tidsskrift for sprogvidenskab*, vol. 3 (1929) pp. 1-20. Repr. in *Studier i norsk språkhistorie*, Oslo 1934, pp. 1-14.

[14] The most recent discussions on *Brávallaþula* are in *Saxostudier* (cf. above note 5), where K. Hald supports Seip's views (pp. 79-90, 93-94) and Stefán Karlsson argues forcibly for the Icelandic origin of the poem (pp. 91-93).

[15] *Scriptores minores historiæ Danicæ medii ævi*. Rec. M.Cl. Gertz, vol. 1, Copenhagen 1917-18, p. 96.

[16] Op.cit. *(Scriptores minores)* pp. 34-53.

[17] GD 100,24-25.

[18] AXEL OLRIK. *Kilderne til Sakses oldhistorie*, vol. 1, København 1892, p. 116.

[19] BJARNI GUÐNASON. *Um Skjöldungasögu*, Reykjavík 1963, pp. 159-161.

[20] Op.cit. pp. 197-200. – INGE SKOVGAARD-PETERSEN. 'Gesta Danorums genremæssige placering', *Saxostudier* pp. 23-24.

[21] Op.cit. *(Um Skjöldungasögu)* pp. 278-283.

[22] INGE SKOVGAARD-PETERSEN. 'Sven Tveskæg i den ældste danske historiografi', *Middelalderstudier tilegnede Aksel E. Christensen*, København 1966, pp. 1-38.

[23] *Sǫgur Danakonunga*, pp. 165-195.

[24] BJARNI GUÐNASON. 'Saxo och Eiríksdrápa', *Nordiska studier i filologi och lingvistik. Festskrift tillägnad Gösta Holm*, Lund 1976, pp. 127-137.

[25] See *Eiríksdrápa*, verse 9, and GD 333,18-21.

[26] GD 445,5-446,32.

[27] BJARNI GUÐNASON. 'Fyrsta sagan', *Studia Islandica* (Reykjavík 1978) pp. 55-66.

[28] *Sǫgur Danakonunga* p. 218.

[29] BJARNI GUÐNASON. 'Aldur og uppruni Knúts sögu helga', *Minjar og menntir. Afmælisrit helgað Kristjáni Eldjárn*, Reykjavík 1976, pp. 55-77.

ORDER IN GESTA DANORUM AND ORDER IN THE CREATION[1]

KURT JOHANNESSON

University of Uppsala

"His force is often misguided and his work shapeless; but he stumbles into many splendours"[2]. This verdict by the English scholar F.Y. Powell may be allowed to summarize the general view of Saxo for the last hundred years. One of the most characteristic features of *Gesta Danorum* is said to be the loose texture of the work, the lack of any rational order or artistic composition. It certainly has its splendours – but Saxo has stumbled into them.

Different ideas have contributed to this evaluation. It was said in the 19th century that Saxo was the prototype of a naive genius. He loved the songs and tales of his people, as he listened faithfully to the memories of his beloved master, Archbishop Absalon. He then started to write it all down without a real plan, but now and then indulging in his own deplorable taste for the artificial, florid Latin of classical poets and medieval scholastics.

It was also said that Saxo must have worked on his history for a very long time. Many scholars tried to establish the exact order in which he had written the sixteen books or even the different parts of them. This genetic method of analysis reached its height or its excess with Paul Herrmann, who also tried to read Gesta Danorum as the spiritual autobiography of Saxo. He had started with his own age and the last books, where the style still reflects a young and realistic mind. Later on he had a new idea, the depiction of Danish antiquity, now writing with a taste for learned speculations and a more rhetorical, florid style. Finally he made a rather unsuccessful attempt to link the different parts together, writing the books in the middle of the work, where his verbal force and moral vigour are sadly slackened by old age.[3]

This theory is based on supposed changes in the language and the stylistic ideals of Saxo – even changes in his view on man and life. But what do we actually know about Saxo and his literary or spiritual development? And is it really so self-evident that he started with the last books? His colleague and rival, Svend Aggesen, had just written his Danish history starting with the origin of the kingdom – why could not Saxo have embraced the same idea from the very beginning?

In conclusion, I find it extremely difficult to prove anything about the chronological order of the different parts of Gesta Danorum. But I think that Saxo at a certain moment had an idea for a scheme that would give his history a rational order and harmonious unity. This method of composition is important for an understanding of Saxo's artistic skill and intellectual background as well as the political and ideological message in his work.

Gesta Danorum is divided into sixteen books. They have roughly the same length, except the huge fourteenth book. Twelve or twenty-four had meant a connection with the tradition from Homer and Virgil – sixteen seems to be a meaningless number. The division into books has also been regarded merely as a mechanical and superficial arrangement of the material. Still, I would maintain that Saxo tried to compose each one of the sixteen books as a thematic and structural unit.

It has been said that the Middle Ages had no real interest in literary composition.[4] But the poetics of the 12th century, the age of Saxo, contain a rather detailed discussion on how to give a simple narration a more artistic composition, an *ordo artificialis*. The author might start with a proverb, a *sententia* or an example to indicate the general theme of the text but also to prepare the audience for the central, decisive part of the story.[5]

This is exactly the technique Saxo adopted in all the sixteen books, even the fourteenth with its immense and puzzling length. The thirteenth book may serve as an illustrative example. It deals with the reign of Niels (1104-34). For Saxo and his age Niels himself was of less interest; the crucial point was the struggle between his son Magnus and his nephew Knud Lavard. Magnus killed Knud in the forest of Haraldsted in 1131 but was himself killed by the men of Knud's brother Erik at Fotevig in 1134. Niels was slain the same year in Slesvig. Different political parties would hail both Knud and Magnus as martyrs and claim that their descendants had the moral and legal right to the throne.

These are the questions Saxo had to answer. But somewhat surprisingly he starts the book with a little story about the unknown Inge, the second son of Niels. As a boy he tries to mount a rather wild horse. His teacher lets him take the reins, but the horse throws him to the ground and tramples the noble boy to death in the dirt of the road.[6] It is easy to pass over this episode as totally insignificant; it may also support the idea that Saxo has written down everything he heard in a haphazard way. But on closer examination it can be observed that the image of the horse and its rider turns up in every important scene in this book. You may even say that Saxo has condensed all the themes, moods and conflicts of the thirteenth book in this opening scene.

The horse and its rider obviously stand for a new military technique, the use of cavalry. Saxo demonstrates how the Danes are now trying to adopt this novelty from the more advanced countries of the Continent.[7] The horse and its rider also stand for a new social class, the knights, who serve the princes by their own skill in this form of battle and by the horsemen they may equip and pay for. The horse and the rider are at the same time the perpetual symbol for the political ruler, the prince, in his effort to dominate the people.[8] The symbol may at last be read on a purely moral level. The horse and the man with the reins in his hand are the ancient image of reason, *ratio,* controlling the passions and desires, i.e. the virtue of *temperantia.*

Saxo has used all these meanings in the most subtle way to give his view on the political issues in the thirteenth book. From the very beginning Knud Lavard, the father of Valdemar the Great, seems to be the indisputable and blameless hero of the drama. Saxo composes a couple of magnificent scenes just to demonstrate Knud's superb skill in fighting on horseback as well as his courtly manners according to the Continental style and his noble *temperantia* in acts and speech – he becomes the very first knight in the Danish history.[9] But he rides to his own death in the forest of Haraldsted, in spite of all warnings. Here Saxo suggests a deficiency, a lack of prudence. The teacher of the young prince Inge was devoid of the same virtue, when he let the unfortunate boy take the reins too early. And when the three princes of the book, Knud, Magnus and Niels, all lie on the ground trampled to death, they are in different ways victims of the same lack of prudence.

Where is this rare virtue to be found? Another scene may give us the answer. After the murder of Knud Lavard, his brother Erik accuses Magnus and his father Niels at the popular court as guilty of the deed.

When the people get to know that Niels refuses to defend himself at the court, law and order break down and an infuriated mob sets out to kill the king. The frightened Niels sends Archbishop Asser to meet the people. Erik rides at the head, but the archbishop catches his reins and forces him and the mob to pull up. And so great is their veneration for the nobility of Asser and the authority of his holy office that the people restrain their wild, destructive movement forward and accept a return to the legal order of courts and laws.[10] Prudence is ultimately to be found with the men of the church; they alone can prevent the destruction of society when prince and people – the rider and the horse – reveal their moral weakness.

It is possible to prove that each of the sixteen books is composed in the same way as a texture of specific themes and symbols. They are usually interwoven in the very first lines of the book in a seemingly casual way. They run through a series of variations and gain a still deeper and more complicated meaning by patterns of opposition and synthesis. They may in some cases reach their ultimate explanation in a final, dramatic scene.

Let me give some examples. The first scene in the fourteenth book depicts how king Erik Emun hesitates as to whether he shall accept the oath of fidelity from his nephews or sentence them to death as traitors. The same hesitation and uncertainty pervade the whole book with a bitter and disillusioned atmosphere. The fifteenth book starts with the superb picture of Bishop Frederik of Slesvig, sailing through the gale and storm to fulfil his duty to the king but being sadly drowned with all his men – a *figura* of the storm Archbishop Absalon has to bear later in this book during the uprising in Scania. The first sentence in the sixteenth book says that Knud must hurry to seize the power after the death of his father Valdemar. The same hurried movement returns in endless variations throughout this book.

Each book has its own leitmotifs and its peculiar atmosphere and internal order. But the different books are also linked together by various schemes. One of them seems to be the pattern of the four cardinal virtues.

The first book starts by saying that the Danes elected Dan and Angul as their leaders for the glorious merits of their bravery, *ob egregia fortitudinis merita.* [11] The rest of the book may appear to be an extremely loose succession of episodes, tales, and songs, fragments of an archaic and mythical world. But one might discover a unifying principle even in this chaotic mass: most of these episodes are actually *exempla fortitudinis,* selected to illustrate different aspects of this virtue. The second book means a change and a new development of this moral theme. The young Frode has inherited the throne, but the wars of his father have emptied the treasury. He fights alone with a dreadful dragon and uses its hoarded gold to pay his warriors. This exemplifies the virtue of generosity, *liberalitas,* the opposite of greed or *avaritia* and, according to the Middle Ages, a part of *iustitia.* Most of the scenes in the second book are there to emphasize the necessity of joining *fortitudo* with this noble *liberalitas.* The third book introduces a new type of prince. He fights as much with the sword as with the tongue and the intellect, and stands for the union of *fortitudo* and *prudentia,* with the revenging Amlet as the true incarnation of these two virtues. But in the fourth book we are to witness the fall and death of Amlet – why? With all his gifts, he lacks one of the cardinal virtues, *temperantia.* His counterpart in this book will be the silent and despised Uffe, who however displays a masterly and tempered bravery in his famous duel with the Saxon prince and his warrior.

The first four books, then, demonstrate how *fortitudo* might and should be united with the other cardinal virtues, that is *iustitia, prudentia,* and *temperantia.* By following this sort of analysis, it is possible to show how the next four books are dominated by *temperantia.* This virtue is the secret of Erik in the fifth book and his instruction of king Frode. This is the virtue that the warrior Starkodder incarnates in the sixth book in his fight against luxury and gluttony, and this is also the virtue of the noble virgins in the seventh book. Thorkil, leading king Gorm and his men through the dangers and horrors in the world of the giants, is the last heroic example of this *temperantia.* But in this book, the eighth, all men – even Thorkil – fail in this virtue. This is the dark, pessimistic book where man is revealed as a foolish, destructive, false and lustful creature – until the old woman Gambaruk prevents a holocaust with a new word and a new virtue: *pietas.* This virtue was in the Middle Ages regarded as a part of *iustitia,* and from the ninth book to the twelfth, Saxo now demonstrates the different forms of this *pietas:* the sense of love and fidelity that unites Ragnar Lodbrok and his sons, a higher obligation towards the country and the people demonstrated by Knud the Great and his men, and finally the *pietas* that contains and consummates all other forms of this virtue, the love for God and the will to obey his law.

I admit that these moral patterns are more complex in the last four books. But it is rather obvious that Saxo in these books gives the last of the four cardinal virtues, *prudentia,* a new and decisive role.

How should this remarkable scheme be explained? I think that Saxo primarily took the idea from the *De officiis* of Cicero and other moral and political treatises based on this model, the so called "mirrors of princes". They combine a systematic analysis of the four cardinal virtues and their parts with examples from the poets and the historians. Saxo has deliberately remoulded the Danish history to give a similar instruction in moral and political wisdom.

This fourfold scheme also corresponds to the fourfold pattern discovered by Inge Skovgaard-Petersen.[12] She has shown that the first four books coincide with the Pagan epoch of world, the four following books with the Christian age outside Denmark, the next four books with the gradual conversion of the Danes and the last four with the Archbishopric of Denmark.

It may be that Saxo also drafted his history as an image of the necessary development of man and society. He starts with *fortitudo* as the most primitive virtue, endowed by nature as a strength to fight for survival, for power and glory. He tries to prove that *temperantia* and *iustitia* – that is, the respect for moral obligations and laws – may give a new ripeness. *Prudentia* is obviously meant to be the last stage of this moral development, providence looking for the ultimate consequence of every human act, wisdom leading the other virtues and discerning between false and true values. On another level of interpretation *fortitudo* may seem to correspond to the function of the princes in society as *temperantia* to a rising class of noblemen. *Iustitia* is above all upheld and fulfilled by the bishops and church and *prudentia* by those faithful and wise counsellors who emerge in the last four books for the rescue of the princes and the whole state. In this way the composition of Gesta Danorum may demonstrate the ideal order both in the human mind and in modern society according to Saxo.

Gesta Danorum may also be read as an allegory of human language and the *artes liberales.* There is in the first book a rather puzzling story about Hading. This Danish prince lives as a boy among giants in Sweden. But the day comes when he wants to leave them to gain the martial glory of his fathers. The giantess Hartgrepe then tries to hold him back with the temptations of love. On his objecting that her body is too big, she describes her endless ability to expand or contract this body at her own will;

first she speaks in prose and then, to achieve more effect, in poetical language.[13] The scene depicts the contrast between the civilized and virtuous Denmark and the barbarian Sweden, a recurring political theme in Gesta Danorum. It also shows the force of magic, another important theme in the first book. On the moral level the scene is meant to describe the eternal struggle of virtue and lust. But Hartgrepe also symbolizes the admirable flexibility of human language and, above all, the various schemes for *amplificatio* and *abbreviatio* developed by the medieval grammarians, that is, the various figures used to give a thought a richer or more concentrated form. On closer examination it will be seen that several of the poems and speeches in the first book demonstrate how a single phrase might be varied according to this technique, for instance a long speech of the enraged Ulfhilda at the end of the book.[14] There is also a striking number of etymological explanations in this book, and many poems where simple metres gradually develop into more complicated poetic patterns. You might say that this book describes the birth of a Danish state and of human virtue as well as the genesis of human language through grammar, the first one of the *artes liberales* and the mother of them all according to the Middle Ages.

The second book starts with the fight of Frode and the dragon mentioned before. When Saxo describes the dragon with its poisoned tongue, its sharp teeth and curling tail, he obviously tries to remind the reader of Martianus Capella, who depicted the goddess of Dialectic with similar phrases and attributes. The first part of the second book is also composed as a series of dialectical duels, demonstrating the different types of arguments or *loci* to be used in disputes.[15] We have reached the second of the *artes liberales,* logic or dialectic.

The leading actors in the third book are Høder and Amlet. The former seems to overcome all human beings with his soft, charming eloquence,[16] the latter fools his enemies by enigmatic words and deeds. This is obviously meant to show the two parts of rhetoric, the play with the emotions as well as the more intellectual and dangerous strategies of sophisms. The first three books, then, bring forth the three *artes dicendi* as they followed each other in the curriculum of the medieval school and in the solemn procession of the *artes liberales* in the poem by Martianus Capella.

But each one of the following books also contains a discussion of specific forms of expression and other linguistic problems. In the fifth book we meet the dispute and the *sententia* or proverb that Erik always uses for his instruction of Frode and his court. In the sixth book Starkodder excels in praise and satire as he does in other forms of moral instruction; the eighth book demonstrates how this aim could be fulfilled by the art of allegory. The following four books are composed according to the different *genera* or cases in rhetoric, such as *genus honestum, anceps, admirabile* and *humile*. Saxo has indeed deserved the name of Grammaticus: no one could give us a more detailed and vivid image not only of the wealth and grandeur, but also of the moral ambiguity of human language.

In this way Saxo has composed a work that may be read – at least in some parts – on three levels, corresponding to history, moral philosophy and the arts of language. But there is still another level, nature itself. There are some allusions to the sciences of the *quadrivium* in different books. The geographical introduction refers to geometry with phrases borrowed from Martianus Capella. The fifth book has a striking number of arithmetical operations. The sixth book contains some hints on astronomy and the seventh may reflect music in its medieval form of mathematical speculation. There are also indications that Saxo tried to combine each of the first eight books with one of the planets, most conspicuously in the last ones referring to the specific qualities and influences of Mars, Jupiter and Saturn.

But Saxo has also been attracted by the Platonic cosmology, which gives some parts of his work its most subtle charm and meaning. In the dialogue mentioned above, the giantess Hartgrepe proclaims that she has a waxen face or shape.[17] This is the conventional Platonic symbol for matter in its original, chaotic and shapeless state. The world comes into being when the ideas descend to imprint their forms on this soft matter. This may also be described as the union of the male and female principles in the universe. This trial of strength between Hading and Hartgrepe, as with many other love stories in the first books, might be interpreted as an allegory of this universal tension between order and chaos in the Creation.

This corresponds to another tension in the work, the tension between the wild profusion of matter and the mathematical rigour of the form. The eighth book is evidently meant to be the centre and focus of the work, like the sixth book in the middle of the *Aeneid;* they both have the same allegorical tale of Man descending to the infernal regions and discovering the Almighty. But the sixteen books are also arranged in four parts, corresponding to the four cardinal virtues and the four stages in the history of Denmark and every human society. In some parts of the work, especially in the first eight books, Saxo has obviously attempted to tell his story on four levels: history, morals, language, and nature. But this magnificent architecture is combined with a sort of musical counterpoint. Vilh. Andersen rightly emphasized the frequence and importance of "gjentagelsen" or the repetition throughout the work.[18] These repetitions of single phrases or characters and scenes are obviously intended to give the different parts a deeper signification through such echoes. But they also strengthen our impression of standing in front of a work or a world obeying its own laws.

It is very likely that Saxo started with a more common plan and by degrees detected the hidden possibilities of the theme. It is most possible that he never had the time nor the strength to fulfil this ultimate scheme. Still, this ideal composition might give us a new point of departure for discussing the spiritual background and personality of Saxo as well as the political and social forces he tried to analyse and master with his work.

This composition points above all to the church and the learned schools of the Middle Ages. The idea of a universal order, created by God and regulated by numbers and measures, was well established by the Fathers. They also accepted the Platonic cosmology as a sort of pagan anticipation of Christian doctrine.

Every grammarian in the Middle Ages, expounding Virgil or Martianus Capella, taught his pupils to look in the myths for the battle of virtues and vices, the four elements, and the stages of human life. The famous grammarians of the French schools in the 12th century gave this exegesis a new, soaring flight, combining these mythological interpretations and the Platonic cosmology with their own passionate interest in the secret laws of language.

These two traditions seem to run into each other in Gesta Danorum. And yet I would underline the originality of Saxo. Other historians of the 12th century refer to the cardinal virtues as the supreme instrument for judging and explaining human characters and actions. But Saxo uses them as supporting pillars for his composition. Other grammarians, e.g. Bernardus Silvestris and Alanus ab Insulis, write allegorical poems about the descent of the soul into the world of matter and its spiritual journey to maturity and salvation. But Saxo takes up the rather intractable material of old Norse tales and Danish history to retell this eternal myth. There is, above all, this incessant speculation on the art and nature of language. For Saxo it is a world of its own, where the transformations and combinations of the words reflect and explain all the processes which constitute the spiritual and physical world, as language itself is an eternal battleground for good and evil. With this belief in the supreme power of language Saxo is bound to attract some readers and give offence to others – and to be a modern writer for any age groping for an ideal order in creation.

[1] This paper is an attempt to sum up certain ideas in my study *Saxo Grammaticus. Komposition och världsbild i Gesta Danorum,* Stockholm 1978 (Lychnos-Bibliotek, 31). For a more detailed discussion and documentation I must generally refer to this work.

[2] *The first nine books of the Danish history of Saxo Grammaticus.* Transl. by Oliver Elton. With some considerations on Saxo's sources, historical methods, and folk-lore by Frederick York Powell, London 1894, p. XXII.

[3] PAUL HERRMANN. *Erläuterungen zu den ersten neun Büchern der dänischen Geschichte des Saxo Grammaticus,* 2 vols., Leipzig 1901-22, passim.

[4] "À la vérité, la composition n'a pas été le souci dominant des écrivains du moyen âge". EDMOND FARAL. *Les arts poétiques du XIIᵉ et du XIIIᵉ siècle,* Paris 1924 (Bibliothèque de l'École des Hautes Études. Sciences hist. et philol., 238), p. 59.

[5] FARAL pp. 55-59.

[6] *Gesta Danorum* (GD, ed. Olrik/Ræder 1931) 342,18-23.

[7] GD 343,7-31; 364,28-35.

[8] GD 344,33-38.

[9] GD 346,19-21 & 29-32; 347,33-38; 351,11-353,4; 355,1-35.

[10] GD 357,13-37.

[11] GD 10,6.

[12] INGE SKOVGAARD-PETERSEN. 'Gesta Danorums genremæssige placering', *Saxostudier.* Red. Ivan Boserup, København 1975 (Opuscula Graecolatina, 2), p. 25.

[13] GD 21,1-22,16.

[14] GD 16,31-17,6; 24,10-14; 32,16-23; 33,1-34,27. It is a striking fact that these *amplificationes* and *abbreviationes* are usually delivered by women. They may be regarded as variations of the goddess Grammatica, but they also suggest the connection between the flexibility of language and that of matter, the female principle in the Platonic universe.

[15] GD 37,6-24; 40,9-41,40; 43,34-45,30.

[16] GD 63,14-17; 65,17-18 & 34-36.

[17] GD 22,8.

[18] VILHELM ANDERSEN. *Tider og Typer af Dansk Aands Historie. Erasmus,* vol. 1, København 1907, p. 66.

AN *EIRÍKS ÞÁTTR MÁLSPAKA?*
SOME CONJECTURES ON THE SOURCE OF
SAXO'S ERICUS DISERTUS

JOAQUÍN MARTÍNEZ-PIZARRO

Oberlin College, Ohio

Of the legendary books of Saxo's *Gesta Danorum,* the fifth is perhaps the most complex; it covers a wealth of historical, legal, and fictional subject-matter, and it seems to have been hastily put together, so that many absurdities and narrative loose ends are to be found in it.[1] In his commentary of 1922 to the legendary part of the *Gesta,* Paul Herrmann analysed the sources of Book V in literature and legend, pointing out the most evident defects in its logic and composition.[2] In the following pages, I would like to take the analysis a few steps further and examine the first three chapters of the book in detail, so as to reveal every single contradiction and break of logical and stylistic continuity. On the basis of these flaws, which will here be listed by letter from A to T, I shall attempt to draw an outline of Saxo's main source and to recover its account of the career of Ericus the Eloquent. I shall also try to trace Saxo's hand at work refashioning his materials, and to explain his aims and the logic of his conception.

Though my conclusions differ in some respects from those of Paul Herrmann, this analysis is based on his work and assumes many of his points of view implicitly, in particular the Icelandic origin of the story of Ericus, and the inexistence of those legends of the Norwegian coast which Axel Olrik took to be Saxo's source.[3]

The study of lost sources is by necessity conjectural; it involves the dangerous but unavoidable premise that stories are quite logical in their earliest version and that all absurdities are introduced in the retelling, so that the form of a source may be discovered by removing contradictions and illogicalities. There is no conclusive proof in an analysis of this kind; the hypothetical source is a construct the persuasive power of which depends entirely on the tightness of the reasoning behind it. My arguments here will be based predominantly on internal evidence; at certain points, however, they will also draw on our general knowledge of the vernacular genres and themes of medieval Scandinavian literature.

In the first half of Book V, the narrative is focused on the career of Ericus the Eloquent. For an analysis of the sources and composition of Saxo's tale of Ericus, we must isolate five segments:

1. the account of the sorry state of the Danish court during the minority of Frotho the Peaceful (Frode Fredegod),

2. the *Brautwerbung* or matrimonial embassy for Frotho's first wife, the Hunnish princess Hanunda,

3. the story of how Ericus became eloquent and visited the king of Norway,

4. the story of Ericus's journey to Denmark and of his reformation of Frotho and the Danish court.

5. Ericus's *Brautwerbung* for Frotho's second wife, the Norwegian princess Alvilda.

Ericus has come down in tradition as "inn málspaki", "the eloquent"; the point of his story is the display and use of his wonderful gift, so that those episodes in which he shines only with other, more ordinary accomplishments, may be reasonably suspected of being late additions to the tale. In segment 5 Ericus, sent by Frotho to Norway to ask for Alvilda's hand, shows a certain ingenuity but is at no point called on to make use of his verbal skills. Segment 5, therefore, falls outside the scope of this analysis.[4] Segments 3 and 4, on the other hand, must be considered the core of Ericus's story, since it is there that our hero gives the most varied demonstrations of his rhetorical powers and his wit.

Segments 1 and 2 are contained in the first chapter of Book V, and their relevance to our subject may seem doubtful, since Ericus appears for the first time in the following chapter. However, the high point of segment 4 is the hero's revelation to Frotho of the adulterous relation between his wife Hanunda and Grep, his favorite counselor. In getting Frotho married, segment 2 is also preparing the scene for this greatest triumph of Ericus. In making Grep and Gøtwara Frotho's agents in the first *Brautwerbung,* segment 2 plays an essential part in the story of Ericus, as these two are to become his most dangerous enemies in 4.

But what about segment 1? Within Chapter 1, it seems inextricably tied to the *Brautwerbung,* since it describes the families of Gøtwara and

Grep, and can also be said to set the scene for the decadent court which Ericus will later reform. Ericus does confront and destroy in 4 many of the corrupt courtiers introduced in 1. However, there are several logical gaps between 1 and the rest of the narrative:

A. Ericus's confrontations in 4 with most of the villains introduced in 1 do not involve the use of rhetoric, while Gøtwara and Grep, both required by 2 (the former as head of the matrimonial embassy, the latter as seducer of the queen) confront the hero in *sennur,* exchanges of invective in which they are defeated.

B. Some of the characters introduced in 1 have important functions or peculiar attributes, yet they are mentioned only once, early in Chapter 1, and do not play a role in the narrative that follows. Westmarus has twelve sons, three of whom are named Grep, yet of these three Greps only one has a part in the story. Isulfus and Aggo are guardians to Frotho and regents during his minority; they are mentioned early in 1 and never again.

C. In 1, Grep attempts to seduce Gunwara, Frotho's sister, and makes her life miserable when she will not give in to his demands. In 2, however, he seduces Hanunda, Frotho's first wife. The persecution and attempted rape of Gunwara never reach a critical point, and there is a clear impression that one narrative thread has been left in the air for the sake of another rather similar one.

D. There seems to be a break between our image of Frotho in 1 and in the following segments. In 1 he is the child-king, with guardians and a regency council; he does not wish to marry on account of his tender age (*teneritudo aetatis),* and his counselor Grep betrays him by attempting to seduce his nubile sister. The *Brautwerbung* and Ericus's visit, however, require a king who can bear the brunt of a debate with "the Eloquent" throughout segment 4, who has given laws (iii. 9 *ne ipse legis a se latae statutum solveret,* "not to relax the statute of the law which he had passed"), whose guardians and regency council are nowhere in sight, and who is sinned against by adultery. It is also the Frotho of segment 4, a king no longer childish, who asks Ericus to obtain for him the hand of the Norwegian princess.

E. The dividing line between 1 and 2 (V.i.5) is marked by a striking change of narrative style. From the elaborate picture of court life given in 1, which involves a multiplicity of offices and dignities, we turn to the world of the *märchen* or *lygisaga,* where descriptions of royal courts often reflect the circumstances of a modest household: here the king of Denmark must get married so that his queen may mend the torn garments of the Danish warriors. For a *fornaldarsaga* with certain historical pretensions, this is a remarkable drop in level.

F. Gøtwara and Grep, whose participation in the tale is assured by their roles in the *Brautwerbung* of 2 and by their *sennur* with Ericus in 4, have been incorporated into 1 by being made relatives of the corrupt ministers and counselors introduced there. Gøtwara is the wife of Colo, one of Frotho's instructors, while Grep is the son of Colo's brother Westmarus. Gøtwara and Grep are therefore aunt and nephew. In 4, however, the relation has changed. As wife of Colo, Gøtwara was the mother of three sons, who are never mentioned after 1. After Grep and his eleven brothers, all supposedly Gøtwara's nephews, have been killed by Ericus and his men, Saxo describes Gøtwara as *consumptae infeliciter subolis exitio maesta simulque eam ulcisci avida* ("sorrowing at the destruction of her children who had miserably perished, and eager to avenge them"), and refers to Ericus in connection with her as *interfector filiorum* ("the slayer of her sons"). She seems to have become Grep's mother, an oversight which can be satisfactorily explained if we take the family relations outlined in 1 as careless inventions serving to connect the story of Ericus with a traditional image of troubled court life.[5]

Saxo has placed the tale of Ericus, with its preliminary *Brautwerbung,* in a context familiar to him from legendary Danish narratives about Frode Fredegod, a king of the "younger dynasty" of the Scyldings.[6] The setting, the decadent, helpless court awaiting a redeemer, recalls the saga of Ingeld and Starkad, as well as the court of the Scylding Hrothgar before the coming of Beowulf. Saxo has made this setting part of the story of Ericus by making the characters of 1 confront the hero in the course of his triumphal first day at court in 4, but he has not been able to make these characters serve the theme of eloquence that underlies his source. Every contact with the themes or characters of 1 turns Ericus into a very average sort of hero, remarkable for physical prowess and little else: he breaks Westmarus's back, and kills off all his children in the course of a battle on snowshoes over the frozen sea.[7]

In Chapter ii Ericus appears for the first time; we learn how he obtained his extraordinary eloquence, and what it was that made him

decide to visit Denmark. The chapter is marred by a glaring absurdi-
ty: the hero displays his gift and earns the cognomen "the Eloquent"
before eating the magic food that will confer power over words.[8]

In Chapter ii, as we have it, Saxo has carried out only structural
alterations of the source, leaving the text unmodified and unadapted
to the changed narrative.

G. Ericus appears for the first time without being introduced, not even as
"a certain Ericus," and proceeds to give proof of his eloquence with a
florid speech. This anticipation of a later episode is indeed crude, but
Saxo seems to have had in mind further modifications which would
have made the sequence more logical. The Norwegian king Gøtarus,
at whose court Ericus has made this first speech, is particularly struck
by his elaborate rhetoric because *frater siquidem eius Rollerus opinio-
nem iuvenis eximio suae fulgore suppresserat* ("for the young man's
reputation had been kept in the shade by the exceeding brilliancy of
his brother Rollerus"). If, as I assume, the brothers' subsequent return to their rural home, and the hero's acquisition of eloquence there
by eating of the magic food prepared by his stepmother Craca for
Rollerus, reflect episodes that in the source anteceded and made
possible Ericus's brilliant speech at Gøtarus's court, then a simple
inversion of the order of these episodes would have made the brothers
arrive at the Norwegian court with Ericus already in a position of
superiority. That Saxo changes this, letting Rollerus be the more
brilliant of the two up to the very moment of Ericus's speech, indicates that he wanted the hero's entire transformation to take place away
from home, spontaneously, as the debut of a "male Cinderella" on a
prestigious stage. This intention in turn provides a clue to the inversion of episodes, since a spontaneous transformation of this sort, which
recalls in many ways Uffo's sudden revelation of his courage and
intelligence in Book IV, would not have been compatible with the
magic food. When he let Ericus appear for the first time at the moment of his speech at Gøtarus's court, Saxo meant to leave out the
brothers' home background and the story of Craca's cooking altoge-
ther. Later, as an afterthought, he must have realized that these first
episodes of the source story could not be omitted without damage to
the narrative: the Craca of segment 3 also plays an important role in
the Norwegian *Brautwerbung* of 5. Saxo had a fondness for the theme
of the magic food concocted from the slaver of serpents, which he had

used in the story of Balderus and Hotherus in Book III. These may have been some of his reasons for preserving the episode, which he now placed after his own version of Ericus's debut. We are left with two successive acquisitions of eloquence by one hero, another aspect of Book V which speaks for the incomplete, unrevised state of its text.

Paragraphs ii.5-9 describe the brothers' return from Gøtarus's court to their parents' home in Rennesø, ostensibly to collect the equipment needed for a journey to Denmark. The return to Rennesø and this intended expedition to Denmark create certain logical difficulties.

H. The brothers would be going to Denmark in the service of Gøtarus, who plans to invade Frotho's kingdom and needs reliable information on Danish affairs. This is why he lets Ericus and Rollerus recruit among his men a company of warriors to sail with them. How is it then that the leaders of the expedition have to get their equipment and funds *(necessaria tam longinqui itineris subsidia)* at home?

I. The decision to go to Denmark is made by Rollerus, and Ericus only makes up his mind to go along after prudent hesitation. This is no longer fitting now that Ericus has proved his genius; he should be the one to take the initiative.

J. Rollerus's motives in travelling to Denmark are not compatible with his mission as Norwegian spy: *Cuius famae experiendae gratia Rollerus, ut erat exterarum lustrator rerum ignotaque visendi avidus, Frothonis se vovit contubernio potiturum* ("In order to examine this rumor, Rollerus, who was a great traveller abroad, and eager to visit unknown parts, made a vow that he would get into the company of Frotho"). To make sense of these statements, we must assume that they were taken over unadapted from the source. Rollerus's vow to visit Frotho and become a member of his *hirð* must have been made before Ericus's transformation, at the time that the brothers still lived at home in the country, and heard seductive rumors about the great courts of Norway and Denmark. Rollerus, as Craca's beloved son, would take the lead in all important matters. Fascinated by stories of Frotho's court, he decided to join the company of warriors surrounding the Danish king. Ericus, a rather obscure figure in those days, chose to follow on his brothers' steps.

Before leaving home, however, the two young men were properly outfitted by their parents.

K. The buried treasures of their father Regnerus would have been of no use to them if, as Saxo has it, they were planning to travel to Denmark in order to spy for the king of Norway. If, on the other hand, they had been leaving their country home in quest of glory in a great foreign court, their father's *gazae* would have been in place.

L. Craca, wishing to provide Rollerus with an advantage, prepares for him the magic food made from the slaver of serpents. Both Knabe and Herrmann find Saxo's account of this incident hopelessly bungled.[9] According to the text (V.ii.6-9), Rollerus spied on his mother and saw her cook the food, yet at table later it was Ericus who, turning the dish around, ate from the potent black portion that had been set before his brother. Though the episode is carelessly told and perhaps insufficiently motivated, it seems to me to make sense as it stands. Knabe and Herrmann believed that the brothers' names had been transposed twice in this account, but to have this happen twice in one paragraph and never again in the entire book seems too great a coincidence. Rollerus's knowledge of the origin of the food would not have made him eager to eat the black portion rather than the weaker white one: Saxo says explicitly that, not knowing that the snakes were harmless, he did not realize how much strength was being brewed for that meal *(Ignorabat enim innocuam anguium extitisse naturam, nescius quantum illo vigoris epulo pararetur)*. Ericus's appetite, on the other hand, is motivated simply by the invigorating effect of the first mouthful *(interni vigoris effectu epulas aestimans ...)*. More information on the subject would have been prejudicial rather than helpful.

Having acquired the magic gift of eloquence in his country home, Ericus set off with his brother Rollerus to visit the court of Frotho. We may wonder about their reasons for stopping at the Norwegian court on their way there. Could they not have sailed to Denmark directly? Is the episode at Gøtarus's court entirely Saxo's creation? The answer to this last question must be negative. Etiquette and expense at the Norwegian court are the subject of a pointed exchange between the hero and Frotho in segment 4. The young Danish king probes the foreign visitor with questions on the standards of his Norwegian rival, giving Ericus ample opportunity for criticism of Frotho's household. Throughout this scene, Ericus is assumed to be well acquainted with Gøtarus's court, as he makes it his term of comparison. In the source, the Norwegian visit must have served a double function, as preliminary exercise of Ericus's new talents and as a setting for his *nafnfestr,* the earning of name and fame as "the Eloquent." After a number of adventures at sea, Ericus lands in Denmark, in the neighborhood of Frotho's hall. Grep, who knows Ericus's reputation, rides out to meet him on the shore and engages him in a *senna* in the course of which the courtier is led to acknowledge the rumors of his adulterous liaison with the queen. This seashore altercation gives rise to some logical problems in segment 4,

M. Saxo hardly tries to motivate this encounter by the sea. He does not say how Grep came to hear of Ericus's arrival or of his fame. He neglects to mention where the two men met and who else was present at their *senna.* All we are told is that Grep hurried down to the seashore: *festinus ad mare contendit.* Since Grep's self-betrayal apparently had no witnesses, it could not have hurt his standing at court. Saxo is forced to overcome this difficulty by making Grep ride back to Frotho's hall to proclaim his defeat in the *senna: at ubi domum pervenit, tumultuoso clamoris impetu regiam complet verbisque se victum vociferans ...* ("Now when he reached home, he filled the palace with uproarious and vehement clamour, shouting that he had been worsted in words ..."), an obviously absurd course of action.

N. This second act of self-betrayal by Grep leads Frotho later on to ask Ericus about the outcome of the *senna.* The hero answers by accusing Grep and Hanunda of adultery. This is Ericus's first appearance at the Danish court. King Frotho hates him and will twice try to kill him in the remainder of segment 4, yet he is willing to believe the accusations against his wife and his close friend without a moment's doubt.

O. The altercation between Ericus and Grep echoes a number of vernacular phrases and terms of invective, and is certainly part of the source. It contains on Ericus's part several clear allusions to the treacherous servant who deceives his master:

> *Nulla fides fidei vacuo praestanda putatur,*
> *quem rumor sontem proditionis agit*
> (»Men think no credit due to him that hath no credit, whom report accuses of treachery«).

> *Qui dominum fallit, qui foedas concipit artes,*
> *tam sibi quam sociis insidiosus erit.*

Aede lupum quicumque fovet, nutrire putatur
praedonem proprio perniciemque lari
(»He who betrays his lord, he who conceives foul devices,
will be as great a snare to himself as to his friends. Whoso
fosters a wolf in his house is thought to feed a thief and a pest
for his own hearth«).

These last words hit Grep off guard and force him to admit his guilt
implicitly. Ericus triumphs in his final statement:

Decipitur quisquis servum sibi poscit amicum;
saepe solet domino verna nocere suo
(»Whoso asks a slave to be his friend is deceived; often the
henchman hurts his master«).

These remarks are aimed as much at the master as at the servant; they
make little sense in the absence of Frotho. If the *senna* had originally
taken place in Frotho's hall and the culprits had betrayed their guilt in
the king's hearing, Grep with his own words, the queen by her cries
and countenance, Frotho's acceptance of Ericus's charges would be
justified, the words of the *senna* would make more sense, and we
would be spared Grep's unlikely ride back to the court to proclaim his
defeat.

Saxo's displacement of this battle of words to the seashore can be
better understood once we realize that he was trying to expand the
stage of segment 4 in order to accommodate Ericus's numerous displays of eloquence and his clashes with the new characters brought
into the narrative with segment 1 (Colo, Westmarus and his sons.)
The source need only have included confrontations with Frotho,
Grep, and Gøtwara.

P. With the *senna*, Saxo has transplanted another small incident from
hall to seashore. On setting foot on Danish soil, Ericus stumbles and
then comments on this as an omen of good luck. Implicit is the proverb "Fall er fárar heil" (V.ii.2: *sibi in lapsu faustum ominatus even-
tum*).[10] Later, after his altercation with Grep, he arrives at Frotho's
hall and, on crossing the threshold, trips on a slippery hide placed
there by Frotho's unhospitable courtiers. Prevented from falling by

Rollerus, who walks behind him, he quotes the proverb "Berr er hverr á bakinu nema sér bróður eigi" (V.iii.8: *nudum habere tergum fraternitatis inopem referebat*).[11] On both occasions the hero is crossing a border and is about to have his wits and character tested in a hostile environment. The stumble is a reminder of the dangers of the situation, but also of the hero's luck. Though the two stumbles here belong to different types, one being proleptic, the other associated in Norse tradition with the phrase "sem fótr ǫðrum" (as one foot (helps) the other), they serve a common function in this respect and constitute in Saxo's text an obvious duplication.[12] The second stumble must be the original one, since its cause, the slippery hide, is mentioned elsewhere in the story both before and after Ericus's arrival.[13]

The outline of Saxo's source which we can recover from internal evidence therefore runs as follows: Gøtwara and her son Grep carry out a matrimonial embassy for the young King of Denmark. The mother obtains the bride-to-be's consent; later her son seduces the new queen.

Following an initiative of his brother Rollerus, Ericus, a young Norwegian living in the country, decides to go abroad in order to visit the Danish court. Before leaving, Ericus eats some magic food prepared by his stepmother Craca for Rollerus, and becomes prodigiously eloquent.

On their way to Denmark, Rollerus and Ericus visit the court of Norway. There Ericus demonstrates his new abilities for the first time and acquires the cognomen of "the Eloquent." Aware of the brothers' intention to travel further, the king of Norway charges them with a secret mission in Denmark, as spies in his service.

On arrival in Denmark, Ericus and Rollerus proceed to the royal hall, where, by means of *sennur* and other forms of verbal aggression, Ericus discredits Gøtwara and Grep, and reveals to the king the latter's adultery with queen Hanunda. The king gets rid of his former favorites and takes Ericus as adviser and friend. The story revolves on the hero's eloquence, and this emphasis on the power of words must have exerted a strong attraction on Saxo, who was, as we know, very fond of rhetoric and verbal ornamentation. In Ericus's speeches before Gøtarus and Frotho, Saxo has left us the brief *De eloquentia* of a hybrid style that combines a mannered Late Latin virtuosity (e.g. in the speech to Frotho saved from drowning, V.iii.22) with the vernacular taste for obscure puns and allusions (e.g. Ericus's dialogue with Frotho on the journey from Rennesø to Denmark, V.iii.10).[14]

The triumph at court of a stranger newly arrived from the backwoods, who dazzles king and courtiers with his eloquence and wit: we have here a familiar formula of Old Norse narrative, a *þáttr*-type that has been described and studied by Joseph C. Harris in its numerous and varied versions.[15] The type is known as the "king and Icelander" *þáttr*, for in these stories the newcomer to court (usually to the Norwegian court) is always an Icelander. This choice goes in hand with the stereotypical attribution of shrewdness and verbal skills to Icelanders in Norse literature. I would like to suggest that the core of Saxo's source is one of these "king and Icelander" *þaettir*.

In his early treatise on the division of Saxo's sources, Axel Olrik remarked that the *þáttr* stood formally between the *fornaldarsaga* and other saga types.[16] In itself, the "king and Icelander" formula requires a measure of realism, and it is often used in the context of kings' sagas, but the story of Ericus as we have it has absorbed elements of the *stjúpmæðrasǫgur* in segment 3 (Craca and the magic food), and of the fairy-tale in segment 2 (the *Brautwerbung*, the queen needed to darn warriors' clothes and wooed with a magic potion). We have here a *þáttr* that is expanding to become a *lygisaga*. But even *lygisǫgur* respected certain chronological constraints: no Icelander could have been minister to a king of the legendary age. The hero's nationality was changed, and he was made a Norwegian. The Icelandic origin of Ericus would explain certain questions raised by his career:

Q. If Rollerus and Ericus were Norwegians, why did they choose to serve a foreign king rather than Gøtarus?

R. Charged with a mission by the king of Norway, why did they give it up on arrival in Denmark? Why would they have gone into Frotho's service even before the Danish king had given them any reasons to feel grateful to him, or welcome at his court?

S. In segment 5, Ericus and king Gøtarus meet again, and yet not a word is said about betrayal, about the brothers' original mission to Denmark, or about Ericus's Norwegian nationality.

The use of the Norwegian court by an Icelander as a stepping-stone on the way to Denmark has an excellent model in the well-known *þáttr* of Auðun and the bear. There too, the hero prefers the Danish court and has conversations with the king of Norway in which the latter manifests curiosity and feelings of rivalry for Denmark.[17]

We may still wonder whether Saxo, who added segment 1 to his source and changed its narrative sequence considerably, could not also have been the one to expand this *Eiríks þáttr málspaka*. More specifically, the question is whether the tale of the eloquent hero's visit to Frotho (our segments 3 and 4) came to Saxo's hands already preceded by the *Brautwerbung* of segment 2. The parts are too tightly and efficiently joined to have been put together by Saxo for the first time. Besides, Saxo is unaware of an element of continuity between 2 and 4 that can nevertheless be found in the text:

T. In segment 2, Frotho pays Gøtwara for her participation in the matrimonial mission by giving her a remarkable gold necklace which Saxo describes in detail (V.i.6). In segment 4, Ericus confronts Gøtwara in a short and spicy *senna,* and she gages "a heavy necklace" *(torquem magni ponderis)* against his life. Narrative economy demands that the necklace she loses here should be the same one with which she had been paid, but Saxo, who had given the most unnecessary details about this ornament when it first came up, fails to make the connection.

We are left with three versions of the story, the first two of which are constructs:

I. A *þáttr* about the Icelander *Eiríkr inn málspaki* which resembles, along general lines, the story of Auðun and the bear: the hero travels to Norway and from there to Denmark; he profits from his eloquence as Auðun from his good manners. The *þáttr* itself corresponds to my segments 3 and 4. Because of the rivalry between the kings of Norway and Denmark in Saxo, Axel Olrik placed his *fornaldarsaga* of *Eiríkr* in the eleventh century, when the tensions created by Magnus the Good's rule over Denmark might have found an echo in such a story. This date does not seem too early for my *Eiríks þáttr*.

II. The *Eiríks saga málspaka,* a *fornaldarsaga,* probably of the early twelfth century, adds a *Brautwerbung* (segment 2) to the *þáttr,* and changes the nationality of the hero. Something of the *märchen*-like tone of this saga is perhaps to be found in the transition from segment 1 to 2.

III. Saxo's version of the *fornaldarsaga.* Saxo has placed his source within the frame of Danish legendary history by adding segment 1 to it.

He has shifted emphasis from the hero's visit to the Norwegian court, which was the high point of *þáttr* and *fornaldarsaga,* to his visit to the Danish king. Finally, he has expanded Ericus's Danish debut with two sorts of new episodes: those which develop the theme of eloquence present in the original *þáttr,* and those in which the hero fights the villains of segment 1 with more usual physical means.

In his commentary, Paul Herrmann has traced sources and analogues of the various elements in the story of Ericus. I would like to end this paper with observations on another possible source of Saxo's version.

The incidents in Chapters 3 and 4 of the *Historia Apollonii regis Tyri*[18] have many elements in common with the plot of our tale:

  i. In both stories, the young hero sails to a foreign country.

 ii. He walks into the king's palace in spite of frightening signs placed at the entrance to scare him away (the sorcerers' *níðstǫng;* heads of dead suitors over the door of Antiochus's palace: ... *et caput eius in portae fastigio ponebatur).* This particular motif in the *Historia* is even more closely matched by an episode in Grep's persecution of Frotho's sister in segment 1: Gunwara had taken refuge in a fortified building; Grep summoned her many suitors to a banquet, had them all beheaded, *ac deinde conclave, cui puella assueverat, desectis eorum capitibus cingens crudele ceteris spectaculum praebuit* ("and then lind the customary room of the princess with their heads – a gruesome spectacle for all the rest"). This echo of the *Historia* in segment 1 shows that the influence of the late Greek romance on the tale of Ericus did not affect the source but only Saxo's version, since it was Saxo who first joined segment 1 to the rest of the story.

iii. Someone at the king's court has a secret guilt of sexual nature (adultery, incest).

 iv. The hero is challenged to a test of wit *(sennur,* a riddle).

  v. The hero has extraordinary verbal skills. Apollonius is described as *fidens in habundantia litterarum* ("confident in the power of literary learning"), and the phrase may have suggested to Saxo a matching of this king of Tyre with the clever Norwegian adventurer of his main source.

 vi. The challenger, who is the possessor of the sexual secret, reveals his guilt in the very test that he proposes (Grep's self-betrayal in the *senna;* King Antiochus's riddle, which discloses his incestuous liaison with his daughter: *Nam quod dixisti: scelere uehor, non est mentitus: te respice ...* ("For when you said "I thrive on crime," you did not lie; look but at yourself")).

All in all, it is a very full parallel, and yet, apart from the beheading of Gunwara's suitors, it seems difficult to determine for any of these elements in the story of Ericus whether it has been influenced by the *Historia* or reached its present form in Saxo's source already.

---

¹ Quotations from Saxo are taken from the standard edition, SAXONIS *Gesta Danorum*. Rec. et ed. J. Olrik & H. Ræder, vol. 1, Copenhagen 1931. Translations are adapted from *The first nine books of the Danish history of Saxo Grammaticus.* Transl. by Oliver Elton, London 1905 (1. ed. 1894).

² PAUL HERRMANN, *Erläuterungen zu den ersten neun Büchern der dänischen Geschichte des Saxo Grammaticus,* vol. 2, Leipzig 1922, pp. 319-340.

³ HERRMANN pp. 11 & 338.

⁴ HERRMANN p. 337 points out that this segment is unlike the rest of the story in that it refers to no vernacular Scandinavian *Realien*.

⁵ HERRMANN unwittingly registers this contradiction in his summary of the story; in p. 332 he refers to Colo's wife as the "in jeder Art von Wortstreit unerschöpfliche Götwara", and to Grep as one of the sons of Westmarus, the eldest of the three who bear that name. In p. 328, however, he mentions "Götvar, die Mutter der Vestmarssöhne" as taking part in a *senna* with Ericus. "Götwara" and "Götvar" do not correspond to two different names in the Latin text, where the termagant's name is always Gøtwara.

⁶ See AXEL OLRIK, *Danmarks Heltedigtning,* vol. 2, København 1910, passim.

⁷ Though HERRMANN hazards no opinion on the composition of Saxo's source, he treats "Die Zustände am Königshofe" in pp. 322-325 as part of an account of Frotho's youth, and separately from "Die *Eiríks saga málspaka*".

⁸ HERRMANN p. 333.

⁹ *Gesta Danorum* p. 110, notes to lines 4 and 15.

¹⁰ HERRMANN p. 394 quotes instances of the use of this proverb in saga literature.

¹¹ HERRMANN p. 395.

¹² For various narrative contexts of the stumble that shows the importance of having a brother, see SAMUEL SINGER, *Sprichwörter des Mittelalters,* vol. 1: *Von den Anfängen bis ins 12. Jahrhundert,* Bern 1944, pp. 20-22.

¹³ In V.i.11, a passage that belongs to segment 1, though in Saxo's text it comes after the *Brautwerbung* of 2, the barbarous treatment of foreign guests at the Danish court is said to include a trick of placing over the threshold of the hall a slippery goatskin, which, pulled from under the feet of those coming in, causes them to fall: *aliis haedinum incedentibus corium substernentes lubrici tergoris offendiculo per occultum funis raptum incautos subegere gressus* ...In V.iii.12, Ericus, who has already experienced this unhospitable practice, asks Frotho for a hide from which to make snowshoes for himself and his men; the king replies: "He who fell on a hide deserves a hide" *(corium meretur qui corio concidit).*

¹⁴ For the tradition of obscure speeches and veiled references in Scandinavian literature and folklore, see JOSEF SVENNUNG, 'Eriks und Götvaras Wortstreit bei Saxo', *Arkiv för nordisk filologi* vol. 56 (1942) pp. 76-98, esp. 78.

[15] JOSEPH C. HARRIS, *The king and the Icelander. A study in the narrative forms of Old Icelandic prose*, diss. Harvard 1969.

[16] AXEL OLRIK, *Kilderne til Sakses oldhistorie*, vol. 1: *Forsøg på en tvedeling af kilderne*, København 1892, p. 14.

[17] "Auðunar þáttr vestfirzka" in *Vestfirðinga sǫgur*. Björn K. Þórólfsson og Guðni Jónsson gáfu út, Reykjavík 1943 (Íslenzk fornrit, 6), pp. 359-368.

[18] I quote from the *Historia Apollonii regis Tyri*. Rec. Alexander Riese, Leipzig 1893 (revised ed.; repr. Stuttgart 1973).

THE WAY TO BYZANTIUM

A STUDY IN THE FIRST THREE BOOKS OF SAXO'S HISTORY OF DENMARK

INGE SKOVGAARD-PETERSEN

University of Copenhagen

Byzantium

In the index to the text of the Gesta Danorum Byzantium is mentioned almost as many times as Rome, but whereas the latter only occurs in the last half of Saxo's work, the Greek city is the place of events both at the beginning and at the end. Rumours of Absalon's victory on Whitsunday were told in Byzantium, according to some of his friends who were at that time serving in the Imperial guard. When Eric the Good went to Jerusalem on a pilgrimage he stayed in Constantinople where he harangued his fellow-countrymen to remind them of old Scandinavian loyalty to the emperor, who on his side presented the pious Danish king with holy relics. In the 11th century Harald Hårderåde, later king of Norway, had an exciting fight with a dragon during his service in the Varangian guard; a hundred years later king Valdemar the Great liked to show Harald's dragon-knife, which had come into his possession. However, the most prominent part that Byzantium has to play in the Gesta Danorum is in the first three books because the pagan gods, the Æsir, had their chief seat in that city. So Saxo maintains a timeless Danish relation with the Greek metropolis, not only in military but also in spiritual affairs. In order to find an explanation of this theory it is necessary to make a survey of Saxo's mythology.

The thesis

In the course of time many scholars have studied the pantheon of the Gesta Danorum, but most of them have been more interested in the history of Nordic heathendom than in Saxo's work.[1] They have therefore treated the subject in a piecemeal fashion without looking for a meaning in these parts of the Gesta Danorum.

A comparison between Saxo and Snorri is inevitable. Andreas Heusler made this distinction:[2] Snorri wrote systematically in Gylfaginning and Skáldskaparmál and historically in Ynglinga saga, both in a dignified manner; Saxo, on the other hand, seemed to have no clear idea of pagan beliefs and could not refrain from sarcastic or ironic comments.

But is this distinction really so evident? Of course Snorri's Edda is a kind of handbook and Ynglinga saga a tale of the Æsir's origin in Asia and their exodus to Scandinavia where they and their offspring lived as kings, first in Sweden, then in the Vestfold of Norway. In other words, they lived and died as human beings at certain times and in certain places. Obviously Saxo's approach is different, but it is possible to point out important agreements between these two almost coæval Scandinavian writers.

Stylistically Saxo has chosen three different types for his mythological parts: a theoretical one, a mythical one, and ordinary narrative where gods and men live together. The last type is to be found in Books I,II, III, and in Books VI, VII, VIII, with a half-hearted addition in Book IX. The pattern I perceive here with three books of mythology before and three books after Christ is another example of the congruity between the book-division and the Universal History of the Middle Ages. In other words, Nordic heathendom seems to have something in common with Christianity in Saxo's eyes.

Only two myths are told in the Gesta Danorum – or rather, the same myth in the first book is repeated in the third with small variations. Theories about pagan religion appear in Book I and Book VI; the latter is the distinction between Odin and Thor to which I shall return later. For the present I shall confine myself to the prelude to the history of king Hadding, the famous exposition of the three kinds of wizards in ancient Denmark.[3]

As you will remember, the first class were the giants who excelled in strength and size, but although they had knowledge of magic they were defeated by the next class, the *mathematici,* who mastered the *pythonica ars* and were therefore much cleverer than the giants. According to Du Cange both words refer to hidden and rather suspicious knowledge of the future which could make people think that *mathematici* were gods. Of course all church-leaders from Augustine onwards warned against this mistake.[4] The third group descended from breeding between the other two. Who are they? In my opinion Saxo wants them to serve as an excuse for speaking of pagan gods through many centuries: in fact they were mortal, but having inherited the tricks of their ancestors they could deceive people that they were the original Æsir. For instance: if the first Odin was the real one, the Odin of the battle of Bråvalla was a late descendant. In this way Saxo could write about pagan deities of the pre-Christian period without disturbing his readers' conscience. This is historical euhemerism, but a different kind from Snorri's.

In her admirable study of Snorri's mythology the Norwegian professor, Anne Holtsmark, pointed out how deeply Snorri was influenced by his attending a Christian school and studying among other books the famous Elucidarius.[5] To an even greater degree this is the case for Saxo. As he did not write a hand-book, but merged the myths in the chronological narrative, it is difficult to distinguish between the source-material and Saxo's own additions.

The Nordic gods are of course false, but they have powers, good or evil, unknown to ordinary people. Is there a purpose to their being introduced in the Gesta Danorum, or are they merely put in for entertainment or as a "Zeitkolorit" – or even accidentally as part of a traditional story?

In order to answer this question I shall begin with an analysis of the mythological parts of the first three books, and then study Saxo's sources in order to be able to distinguish between the background and the use Saxo makes of it. Finally some deductions may be drawn as to Saxo's ideas.

A. Saxo's text

I. Hadding

The history of king Hadding falls into two distinct parts: his youth and years of learning, and his manhood as a king of Denmark. Between these tvo parts Saxo puts in the myth of the Æsir in Byzantium. Only a very superficial reader can miss the point of this composition.

a. Hadding's youth

As a child and young man Hadding is brought up by giants. His foster-mother and later mistress especially, the giantess Hardgrepa, is a fascinating person. She understands the art of deceiving, but in the end her tricks cause her own death: she places a tablet with a runic spell under the tongue of a dead man thus forcing him to speak; he threatens her with an ugly revenge and suddenly she is gripped by forceful hands and torn to death. The magic of giants is disclosed as pure self-deception. After Hardgrepa's disappearance an old man with one eye takes care of Hadding; he gives him a foster-brother, Liserus, rides with him on horseback over the sea, and later in a poem instructs him how to escape dangers. Among other things he advises him to drink lion's blood in order to become strong and courageous. The old man's advice proves effective, so that the difference between the arts of giants and those of the new teacher – Odin of course – is apparent. During his adventures in the Eastern Baltic Hadding succeeds in conquering the town of Dünaborg by means of a cruel ruse. He receives ransom so that he is able to raise an army against Svipdag, the king of Sveden and Denmark. In a battle Hadding carries the day and becomes king of Denmark.[6]

b. The Æsir

Here the tale of the gods in Byzantium is inserted.[7] We are prepared for it first by Odin's appearance, then by Hadding's raid along the Düna, one of the river-roads through Russia and via the Black Sea to Constantinople, alias Byzantium. The meaning of the ensuing story of Odin's misfortunes is to warn the reader against believing that this man was a god. Only superstitious Scandinavian kings could think so. If they had seen him in his own surroundings they would have laughed at a husband with a wife like Frigga, and at his subsequent exile. Just as ridiculous was Odin's substitute, Mithodin, who brought nothing but harm to his new home in Fyn when he was expelled from Byzantium. The inhabitants of the island had to get rid of his plague-stricken corpse by planting a stake through it. And we now understand why this myth is placed in this context and how it could be that Odin dwelt by the Baltic Sea at the time of Hadding's youth during his exile from Byzantium.

c. Hadding's reign

The last part of Hadding's history from his succession to the throne to his death must be seen in the light of Odin's teaching. Still, it is rather difficult to find a connection between the many anecdotes. If we look closely, however, it is possible to detect at least two entwined threads.

One of them is Hadding's family-history.[8] He marries the daughter of the king of the Nitheri, a people living at the foot of the Jotunheim, home of the giants. Hadding won his bride by killing a giant, and she recognized her liberator by a ring which she had left in a wound in his leg. When married they stayed for a while in Norway. Here Hadding had a curious adventure. A woman came out of the floor with a bunch of poisonous hemlock and asked him to go with her to the place where these plants grew. On his way down he saw men dressed in purple togas and a river seething with weapons. The hemlock grew at the other side of the river where warriors were fighting old battles over and over again. At last they came to a wall. To find out what was behind the wall his companion threw a decapitated cock across it and they heard the revived bird crow: on the other side was eternity.

Apparently the marriage with the Norwegian princess was not happy. She longed for the mountains and forests of her home, whereas Hadding soon became tired of farming and wanted to put out to sea. Still, they had three children, Uluilda who tried in vain to kill her father, Frode who became his successor to the throne and a brave warrior, and Suanhuita, the true heir to Hadding's wisdom.

Before we follow this line into the second book we shall look for another thread in Hadding's life: the continuous war with three genera-tions of Swedish kings. Many curious incidents occurred during these hostilities. For instance when he killed king Asmund he was hurt in his foot and gained a perpetual limp.[9] Once Hadding was defeated and took refuge in Hälsingaland, he came upon a sea-monster which he killed. A woman appeared and told him that all the storms of the world would follow him till he had expiated his deed, because the monster was holy. Hadding hastened to sacrifice black oxen to the god Frø in Uppsala.[10] These rites were repeated as "Frøblot" every year until Frø began to demand human sacrifice instead of the oxen. Whether he was the winner or the loser Hadding always obeyed the orders of the higher ones. His own death is the last and best example of this. Though his relation with King Hunding of Sweden seemed to be good, Hunding was delighted at the false rumour of Hadding's falling prey to his daughter's cunning. Hunding celebrated the event with a large feast where he himself was drowned in a big jar of mead in the hall. Whether it was Orcus, the god of the Underworld who revenged Hadding's supposed death, or whether it was Hadding himself who ordered Hunding's end, we cannot tell. In any case, Hadding decided not to outlive his old adversary and hanged himself on a tree in the sight of his people.[11]

The curious tale of Hadding's adventures is made up of a very complicated source-material, more literary than historical, as I shall later display, but I might just as well make a preliminary conclusion: Hadding was the first Dane to be acquainted with the supernatural world, but he did not understand it. He was dutiful and pious, but every happening he encountered was mysterious or even magical.

II. Suanhuita and Regner

Of his children the most interesting one is Suanhuita.[12] She hears rumours of how shamefully Hunding's widow treats her stepsons, letting them tend cattle in the fields as mere thralls. Suanhuita then rides to Sweden together with her sisters, and finds the princes in poor condition surrounded by a horde of dreadful monsters. Regner, the eldest of Hunding's sons, refuses to see the horrible crowd around him, just as he shuts his eyes to his degrading work. Suanhuita teaches him to stand up like a prince and fight the demons. She gives him a sword and stands by his side for the whole night. At dawn the evil spirits lie dead around them; one of the corpses is Regner's spiteful stepmother.

This story is told so that every reader perceives that it is the task of a king to distinguish good from evil. Previously Regner knew one thing only: that Thor is in heaven; but when Suanhuita made him feel pride in his position as the son of a king he acted as he ought to. (But he did not like his bride to prompt his deed!) I shall return later to Saxo's handling of this text.

III. Hother and Balder

The last story I want you to consider is that of king Hother, which is so complicated that I can only touch upon the most essential points. Hother was a grandson of Regner and Suanhuita and brought up by the wise Norwegian king, Gevar, whose daughter Nanna he wooed and married. His most famous achievement was to gain a victory over the Æsir and especially to defeat Balder both in war and in love. His success was due to inherited gifts and good schooling: he could play many musical instruments and was well trained in several sports. More than that, he listened to good advice and king Gevar taught him how to win a powerful ring and the only sword that could kill Balder by using Nature's gifts: he put up his tent in the shadow of the satyr Miming's grove and attacked the owner of the ring and the sword, when the latter came out in daylight and could not see the white tent in the snow. Most extraordinary was Hother's habit of seeking solitude and staying awake for the night before any important decision was to be made. Three wood maidens would help him when he was on the point of losing his courage.[13] That this setting is one of pure 12th century knighthood is beyond any doubt, as well as the fact that many items of this story are symbols of a growing distrust in the Æsir as representatives of real values.

Therefore Saxo is rather haughty when speaking of Balder's sexual desire and Odin's mean tricks to enable him to rape the Russian princess Rinda, who is to give birth to the revenger of Balder.[14] On the other hand, we believe in Balder's deep love for Nanna, and the spring he discovers for his thirsty soldiers is a Christian symbol. Balder knows all forms of love. Saxo is broad-minded, but nobody can fail to see the irony of the situation when everybody turns to Odin in Byzantium as the only light of the world after the vile deed of raping Rinda. Only Hother and Nanna could see through the false gods. Surely there was still a long way to go before real wisdom came to Denmark.

Though I am quite aware that this audience is well acquainted with the three stories I have retold, it is my hope that looking at them in sequence has disclosed a development, namely from Hadding's magical "Odinized" character – as Georges Dumézil has put it – via Suanhuita's combination of a social and moral outlook to Hother's reliance on himself instead of on the Æsir. The question is, who has invented this evolution?

B. The sources

First I want to maintain that those who believe that Saxo took over a ready-made Nordic composition will have a hard task to prove it. There is not a scrap of evidence of a king Hadding in Denmark, nor a king Hother. Suanhuita on horseback as a valkyrie or "fylgjukona" for Regner is not known from other texts. That does not mean that Saxo wrote out of thin air; we even know some of his sources, or at any rate parallel texts, but they are not dated and appear in other connections.[15] So Saxo seems to have relied on a wide-spread literature, picking out here and there what he wanted for his purpose. If this picture is right, the first eight books of the Gesta Danorum are not history in the modern sense of the word, but a sort of fiction, or, to put it better, Saxo's legendary history represents a different historical reality from what we know nowadays.

I. The history of Hadding

It is an old observation that the dialogue between Hadding and his queen, Ragnhild, closely corresponds to a poem in Snorri's Edda.[16] Here the As Njord marries the giantess Skadi – who by the way chose him because of his handsome legs just as Ragnhild chose Hadding! – but they quarrel about whether life is better on land or at sea. The French historian of religion, Georges Dumézil, begins his study of Hadding's history with this comparison and here finds a key to the personality of the king. I agree, but would interpret the story in another way. Dumézil sees the difference between the farmer and the sailor as a part – an extraordinarily complex part – of his view of Indo-European religion. The main point for me is that Ragnhild and Skadi want to live on terms with Nature, while Hadding and Njord wish to go to sea, seek new horizons, cross old boundaries and make their own fortunes. This ideal is that of the viking; he is the one who was to expand the possibilities of the Danish people.

From this identification we can go on to a highly disputed model of Hadding's person: the viking *par excellence,* Hasting, or as Dudo calls him, Anstignus.[17] Now Dumézil is obviously right when he denies any resemblance between these two names, Hadding and Hasting. But, the names apart, there is a certain similiarity between the two men's acquisition of their realms. Each starts with a viking raid and follows a route ending in the most famous city of his world – Rome and Byzantium respectively – but is held back by an attack on a rich town: Luna and Dünaborg are captured by cunning stratagems. With the ransom they receive from the towns they are able to win the country they first wanted, Normandy and Denmark. This means that they are not only vikings, but men with a vague notion of the highest aim in their world, and when finally they return to their old land they want to carry out their ideals – in Denmark Hadding is an Odin "en miniature"!

To support this theory I want you to notice the correspondence between Hadding's adventures and the deeds which Odin boasts of in the Ljódatal of Hávamál[18] culminating with the famous strophe of his hanging for nine days on a tree in order to gain wisdom. However modern philologists interpret this strophe, I am convinced that Saxo understood the text as an oblique reference to Christ on the cross, just as other biblical as well as classical allusions may be found in Hadding's history. For instance when Asmund before his death hurts Hadding's foot so that from then on he must limp, we are reminded of what the Lord God said to the snake in Paradise: "I will put enmity between thee and the woman, and between thy seed and her seed; it shall bruise thy head, and thou shall bruise his heel ..."[19] Or when Hadding has killed the sea-monster a woman threatens him: "The wrath of the prison of Æolus shall be loosed upon thy head" – meaning that the tempests from all the four corners of the world will pursue him, just as happened to Ulysses and Æneas. But the neatest combination of classical and Christian images occurs in Hadding's journey to the Underworld. Ten years ago at the Saxo-colloquium the late Profesor Teilgaard Laugesen pointed out that this journey was a loan from the sixth book of the Æneid, which is confirmed by many details.[20] Still, Vergil's conclusion of Æneas's visit to the reign of the dead is quite different from Saxo's. The latter thinks here of Christian resurrection: what the cock's crow announced was that behind the wall was the land of life after death – "De Levendes Land" as Grundtvig said.[21]

II. Martianus Capella and the story of Suanhuita

As for the story of Regner and Suanhuita, Stephanius already recognized Saxo's debts to Martianus Capella's book on the wedding of Philology to Mercury.[22] The long list of monsters is exactly the same in the two texts. Again it is not only the names but an idea that Saxo has borrowed from Martianus's second book. Here Juno informs Philology of her journey through the spheres; in the innermost circle round the Earth and under the Moon ugly demons reside seeking refuge in groves and among rocks. They are the evil vices that must be defeated if you want to advance to higher spheres. For Martianus Capella cosmology is identical with the soul of mankind. Reading Suanhuita's and Regner's battle against the evil monsters, we can see that Saxo had the same thoughts about spiritual development. What in Hadding's eyes were magical forces became moral problems to his daughter.

III. Sources for the fight between Hother and the Æsir

Finally: did Saxo know a now-lost version of Balder's death, as is widely maintained? Looking at the many similiarities between the Norse tradition and the Gesta Danorum I am inclined to think of a common origin, resembling the former more closely, and treated very freely by Saxo.[23] The names, Odin, Balder, Nanna and Hother/Hǫðr are identical, and the most important event, the killing of Balder by Hother, is the same in the two traditions – *mutatis mutandis*. In its essence Odin's revenge by the procreation of a revenger corresponds to the Edda poem of Balder's dreams. In fact on this point Saxo seems to be closer to the Norse origin than Snorri with his sublime story of all beings weeping to regain Balder from Hell.

If Saxo did not know more of Scandinavian mythology than we do he has really dealt with it boldly. Instead of the blind, weak Høder who may have been prompted by Loke to take part in the arrow-shooting at Balder, Hother is in the Gesta Danorum a clever and brave king, surpassing even the gods. The plot in the Gesta Danorum is a love-triangle whereas in the Norse version Balder's death is caused by the Æsir's naive *superbia* with a blind faith in the goodness of all beings. On account of this fundamental change, which must have been made by Saxo, many details have been altered. Still, the two versions have the same conclusion: the Æsir were not gods, they were mortals. In a larger perspective there is another coincidence: Vǫluspá and Snorri let Balder's death be the first warning of the coming disaster, Ragnarǫk.[24] In a way Saxo's story points towards the same end: when Hother acknowledged the weakness of his adversaries the first doubt of their divinity had arisen.

Summing up: of course centuries of Saxo-scholarship have not been in vain; the importance of the Norse texts for the Gesta Danorum is confirmed, but Saxo uses them personally and mingles them with Christian and classical conceptions. From his enormous reading he has chosen what fitted his purpose. The last questions are: why were the Æsir introduced into the history of Denmark – and why were their headquarters in Byzantium?

Conclusion

Thor is rather difficult to appreciate in the first books. Regner calls him the only god, but for Hother Thor is no better than the other Æsir: though he made a magnificent appearance in the great battle between gods and men, he was defeated when Hother shortened his axe-handle.

Then in the sixth book the double comparison between Odin and Thor and between Scandinavian and classical mythology is developed. No doubt in these sentences Saxo is warning us against believing in any of the pantheons, but in the details the Roman Jove is rightly placed over Mercury and it is a mistake to let Odin be the father of Thor.[25] On the contrary: Thor has Nature on his side when helping Halvdan Biarggram[26] to hurl stones on the enemy and when chaining Utgardloki[27]. The resemblance to the myth of Prometheus is well calculated: The Greek Titan waged war against the gods by teaching men to use fire, in the same way that Utgardloki was a master of fire. But notice that Thor only used natural means to combat his enemy.

Odin seems at first to be the father of all progress among the Danes; Hadding could not distinguish between the results and their author and died on the tree whereas Odin himself stepped down after nine days' hanging, wiser than before. Odin has knowledge of war strategy, scaldic poetry, runic spells, and any form of dissimulation. In short: he is the teacher of spiritual arts. For better and for worse Odin exemplifies the potentiality of mankind. There is deep understanding between Odin and Danish royalty, but when Hother learns some of his arts, Odin's role changes. All his cleverness is used to prompt people to fight and die – his whole knowlege leads to death; in the battle of Bråvalla and in the figure of Jarimar, a wolf in human form, Odin finds his counterpart, "for he always loved the Danes".

The entwining of stories from classical antiquity and the Bible is characteristic of the renaissance of the 12th century. Saxo added Norse lore to this, and the common idea behind it was that the history of mankind was one, but that the various peoples had attained different stages of understanding before they adapted Christianity.[28]

Why did Saxo place the Æsir in Byzantium? This problem seems to have been resolved long ago. Already Ari let the Æsir come from Asia and wander to Scandinavia at the beginning of history. In Ynglinga saga the origin was moved to Troy, and other Icelandic writers took the last step and began with Miklagarðr=Constantinople/Byzantium. This string of ideas may easily go back to Saxo's time.[29] But Saxo nowhere speaks of an exodus from Byzantium to Scandinavia; apparently they lived now here, now there. There does not seem to be any need for a southern seat.

In the early and high Middle Ages Byzantium/Constantinople was not only a large and a rich city, but it was the metropolis of Greece and famed for learning. We do not know how much Greek culture was studied in Western Europe, even if the term, Greek learning, was highly appreciated. But it had one fault: it was not Christian. On the other hand precisely this fact made it fit for ancient pagan times. For Denmark Saxo could make it really appropriate; quoting Dudo he says at the beginning of Book I: some say that the Danes are descended from the Danai=Greeks *(Danos a Danais ortos).*[30] The quotation is correct, but a look into *De moribus et actis Normanniæ ducum* will convince us that Dudo thought that *Danai* meant Trojans and that the Danes like so many other European people came from Troy.[31] Saxo with his vast reading knew better and quoted only the words that fitted his purpose. Of course he did not believe in the Æsir as gods, but he was well aware that the old Scandinavians did, and he maintained that the Danes grew wiser during their connection with the Æsir in Byzantium because they learned Greek *scientia*. In the course of time this was disclosed as pure human knowledge; the Æsir were abandoned, and the peoples of Scandinavia sought Christian *sapientia* instead. Now Rome became the spiritual metropolis of Western and Northern Europe, but the Danish acquaintance with Byzantium endured on a more equal footing than at the beginning.

[1] JAN DE VRIES, *Altgermanische Religionsgeschichte*, 2 vols., Berlin 1956-57[2] (Grundriss d.germ. Philol., 12/I-II); E.O.G. TURVILLE-PETRE. *Myth and religion of the north. The religion of ancient Scandinavia*, New York 1964; FOLKE STRÖM. *Nordisk hedendom. Tro och sed i förkristen tid*, Göteborg 1961; H.R. ELLIS DAVIDSON. *Scandinavian mythology*, London 1969.

[2] ANDREAS HEUSLER, *Die gelehrte Urgeschichte im isländischen Schrifttum*, Berlin 1908 (Abhandl.d.Preuss.Akad.d.Wiss., phil.-hist.Klasse, Nr. 3), reprinted in his *Kleine Schriften*, vol. 2, Berlin 1969 pp. 80-161 (p. 145).

[3] SAXONIS *Gesta Danorum*. Rec. et ed. J. Olrik & H. Ræder, vol. 1, Copenhagen 1931, I, v.

[4] DU CANGE. *Glossarium mediae et infimae Latinitatis* (Niort 1883-87), vol. 5 s.v. *mathematici.*

[5] ANNE HOLTSMARK. *Studier i Snorres mytologi*, Oslo 1964 (Skrifter utg. av det Norske videnskaps-akademi i Oslo, II: Hist.-filos. klasse. Ny serie, 4).

[6] GD *(= Gesta Danorum)* I,vi.

[7] GD I,vii.

[8] GD I,viii, 13 & 18 & 23-26.

[9] GD I,viii,1-4.

[10] GD I,viii,11-12.

[11] GD I,viii,27.

[12] GD II,ii.

[13] GD III,i-iii.

[14] GD III,iv.

[15] PAUL HERRMANN. *Erläuterungen zu den ersten neun Büchern der dänischen Geschichte des Saxo Grammaticus*, vol. 2, Leipzig 1922, passim.

[16] SNORRI STURLUSON, *Edda*. Udg. af Finnur Jónsson, København 1926², p. 28 (stanzas 30 and 31). Cf. GEORGES DUMEZIL, *La saga de Hadingus. Du mythe au roman*, Paris 1953 (Bibliothèque de l'École des hautes études. Sciences religieuses, 66).

[17] DUDO, *De moribus et actis primorum Normanniae ducum*. Nouv. éd. par Jules Lair, Caen 1865 (Mémoires de la Société des antiquaires de Normandie, 3. ser. 3. vol. 2. partie).

[18] For instance: Odin can heal sickness, blunt swords, deliver people from fetters, catch the spear of an enemy, make a dead man speak by a runic spell and many other things. Sometimes it is Hadding who draws the advantage of Odin's counsel, now and then others master Odin's gifts (especially those of black magic). Hadding's enemy Toste succeeds in causing a disagreement between his fellows where Odin himself prefers to make peace. The point is that unless better sources turn up I consider the curiously unconnected anecdote in the history of king Hadding as Saxo's attempt to write stories from the stanzas of *Ljóðatal*.

[19] Genesis 3,15.

[20] ANKER TEILGAARD LAUGESEN in *Saxostudier*. Red. Ivan Boserup, København 1975 (Opuscula Graecolatina, 2), p. 28.

[21] "De Levendes Land" is the title of Grundtvig's psalm "O Kristelighed".

[22] MARTIANUS CAPELLA, *De nuptiis Philologiae et Mercurii*. Ed. Adolfus Dick, Leipzig 1925, p. 69.

[23] Balder's death is most fully described by Snorri in *Gylfaginning*. Most of the story derives from *Vǫluspá*, stanzas 31-33. Loke's influence is only to be found in Gylfaginning.

[24] Ragnarǫk: Vǫluspá, stanzas 43-58 (Sigurður Nordal's ed., Reykjavík 1923 (Árbók Háskóla Íslands 1922-23)).

[25] GD VI,v,2.

[26] GD VII,i-ii.

[27] GD VIII,xv,8.

[28] I hope to present further studies in this very exciting problem. It has been treated by PAUL RENUCCI in *Dante. Disciple et juge du monde gréco-latin*, Clermont-Ferrand 1954.

[29] HEUSLER, op.cit. p. 146.

[30] GD I,i.

[31] DUDO, chapter 1.

WOMEN IN GESTA DANORUM

BIRGIT STRAND

University of Gothenburg

I. SAXO'S DESCRIPTION OF WOMEN COMPARED WITH SNORRE'S

Gesta Danorum has been the subject of a great many investigations, but none of these has been devoted to its female characters. Yet *Saxo Grammaticus* differs noticeably from older and contemporary northern historians by giving comparatively many detailed descriptions of women. The only historian who in this respect can equal Saxo is *Snorre Sturlason,* and therefore a comparison between these two appears to be a tempting proposition. But no special examination has been devoted to Snorre's female characters either. It is true that the German scholar *Rolf Heller* discusses *Heimskringla* in his *Die literarische Darstellung der Frau in den Isländersagas,* but for my purpose his work is far from sufficient. I have therefore had to complete it with a summary analysis of my own concerning the descriptions of women in Snorre's *Lives of the Norse kings.*

In spite of the fact that Saxo has used much Norse material, it is difficult to find direct parallels in Heimskringla. An episode involving Sigrid "the Strong-minded" is almost an exception. It can be illuminating to study how the same woman is described by different authors: the Sigrid episode forms a starting-point for a comparison between Saxo and Snorre and a closer examination of Saxo's attitudes towards and opinions of women. To start with I shall summarize the Sigrid episode, first Saxo's version, then Snorre's.[1]

Sigrid the Strong-minded in Saxo
King Olav Tryggvason (of Norway) wanted to conquer Denmark and, in order to get the land of Sweden on his side, he proposed to Sigrid, the widow of King Eric the Victorious of Sweden and the mother of Olav

(Ericson). But the Danish king, Swein Forkbeard, would not expose his country to an attack from two sides, and therefore he devised a way to prevent Olav's and Sigrid's marriage. Instead, Olav was coaxed into proposing to Swein's young daughter, Tyri, and the menace of a coalition between Norway and Sweden was removed. But Olav was satisfied:

"He preferred the maiden to the mature lady; he would rather wed the maiden and did not feel at all inclined to waste his fair youth in the arms of a widow. He soon brought to light how little he esteemed the latter, and how much he honoured the former."[2]

Olav sent for Sigrid, pretending that he wanted to talk with her and asked her to come on board his ship. The chaste Sigrid refused at first but later yielded. When she was going on board, Olav let some of his men dislodge the gang-plank so that she fell headlong into the water. The Norwegians were not content with this but made fun of her immorality and profligacy.[3]

The queen came very near drowning and only just escaped to the shore, while the Swedes stood "feeling annoyance" at it all. When she had regained her composure and understood that it had been Olav's intention to expose her wantonness, she could remain silent no longer and "uttered threats" against him in reply.[4]

Thus Swein Forkbeard's guile succeeded in depriving Olav of Sigrid's power and, instead, he won her for himself: he gained her consent all the more easily as she now hated Olav. Swein then revenged his wife's shame by refusing to give Olav his daughter Tyri. The discord between the kings resulted in open war, where Swein obtained help from Sigrid's son, Olav Ericson.

Sigrid the Strong-minded in Snorre

In Heimskringla we meet Sigrid before Olav's proposal and are then given the explanation why she came to be called "the Strong-minded": Sigrid wanted to make the minor kings loathe coming from other lands to woo her. Therefore she invited two of them to a feast in order to burn them at night, when everybody was drunk. Hence her surname. Olav Tryggvason's proposal, however, she took kindly, and after the matter had been agreed upon, Olav sent her a large gold ring. It seemed to be a very costly gift, but when Sigrid discovered that there was brass inside it, she was extremly annoyed and suspected that Olav would betray her in more things than this. Early in the spring Olav came to Konungahella

himself to meet queen Sigrid and speak about their marriage. He demanded that she be baptized and take the true faith, but Sigrid answered:

"'I will not go from the faith I have had before, and my kinsmen before
me. I will not say anything against thee if thou believe in the god that
pleases thee.' King Olav was very wroth and answered hastily: 'Why
should I wed thee, thou heathen bitch?' and he struck her in the face with
the glove he was holding in his hand. After that he stood up and she
likewise and Sigrid said: 'This may well be thy death!' They parted and
the king went north to the Wik and the queen east into Sweden."[5]

Sigrid instead married Swein Forkbeard after his wife Gunnhild, the
daughter of Burislav, King of the Vends, had died. With this new kinship
there arose great friendship between Swein and Olav the Swede, Sigrid's
son.

King Burislav was to marry Tyri, the daughter of Harald and the sister
of King Swein; but the wedding had not been carried out: Tyri had said
'nay' very curtly to being married to a heathen old man. After pressure
Swein, however, gave his sister to Burislav. "Tyri wept and went away
most unwillingly".[6] Soon after the wedding she fled. She came to Denmark but dared not remain there, since she knew that Swein would
immediately send her back to Burislav. Therefore she fled to King Olav
in Norway, "and from him she begged helpful counsel and peace for
herself in his kingdom."[7] When he asked her if she would marry him, she
considered this a good solution. The wedding took place, but soon Tyri
began to complain to King Olav that her great possessions in Vendland
were now lost. She asked Olav to help her regain them, but Olav's friends
all advised him against such attempts. Nevertheless Tyri taunted Olav for
his cowardice with the result that he prepared himself for warfare. Sigrid,
who could not forget Olav's insult, continually egged on King Swein to do
battle with King Olav. Since Olav had wedded Tyri without his assent,
this was a strong enough case for attack, she said. And – like Tyri – Sigrid
succeeded in instigating war: the battle between Olav and Swein was
fought at Svolder (in 1000), where Swein got help from Sigrid's son, Olav
Ericson.

Comparison
Here we get two completely different pictures of Sigrid the Strong-min-
ded and Tyri. Common features are that Olav Tryggvason proposes to
Sigrid, and she accepts. The agreement is broken, Olav insults Sigrid, she

threatens him wrathfully and instead marries Swein Forkbeard. Owing to this the friendship between Swein and Sigrid's son Olav, King of Sweden, is increased. Swein's sister Tyri (his daughter in Snorre) contributes to the enmity between Swein and Olav Tryggvason.

But the differences are more numerous: The authors are on quite different levels when they explain Olav's change of mind, as well as his intention with the insulting treatment to which he exposes Sigrid: Saxo confronts the older woman, the widow Sigrid, with the younger, the maiden Tyri, while Snorre confronts the heathen Sigrid with Olav's Christian faith.

In Saxo Olav acts as a political imbecile, when he, contrary to his original plans, not only voluntarily abstains from marrying the powerful queen, but furthermore rudely insults her. Olav Tryggvason reveals himself as a dishonest brute. His manners are explained as being typical of the barbarian Norwegians – nor is any other reason given by Saxo.

In Snorre the insult, as well as Olav's change of mind, is given a completely different explanation. Here it is no longer the despised older woman who unjustly – and for the fun of it – is dishonoured, but the heathen, who refuses to take the Christian faith. Olav's behaviour is made understandable: in his ardour for extending the Christian faith he could not act otherwise.

In Saxo Swein Forkbeard plays the leading part. It is he who has arranged it all: fearful of an attack from two sides he uses Tyri as a bait in order to prevent a union of Norway and Sweden. He is so sucessful that he himself can marry Sigrid and thus get the Swedish king on his side against – the now isolated – Olav Tryggvason. Snorre does not know this version (so advantageous for the Danes). In Heimskringla it is not Swein Forkbeard but Olav Tryggvason who is the leading actor: it is his Christian conviction that prevents the marriage to queen Sigrid (which can be said to cause his catastrophe). And Tyri is here no bait which is withdrawn but an independently-acting woman, who completely on her own initiative goes to see Olav Tryggvason and marries him. It is the demand for Tyri's possessions in Vendland which impels Olav to warfare and brings him to Svolder – and into the arms of the allied kings, Swein and Olav Ericson.

How are these differences to be explained? – To begin with, the two versions give us the prelude of the battle of Svolder, and *Lauritz Weibull* has shown how two conflicting opinions of the enmity and fight have formed the basis of the different versions which we find in the literature about Olav Tryggvason and his adversaries.[8] The prelude to the battle has been shaped in accordance with one of these opinions: According to the older one, Olav starts the war, and the battle is fought in Öresund: according to the later one, Olav is attacked, and the battle is fought at Svolder.

In *Adam of Bremen,* who gives us the oldest description, it is Tyri who instigates the war, but in the later Norse version Olav is no longer the attacker; thus the inciting role has been transferred to Sigrid, the new attacker Swein Forkbeard's wife.

It is, however, noticeable that Saxo, who agrees with Adam's opinion of Olav as an attacker, does not describe Tyri as the instigator, as Adam does. And further: In Snorre, who, according to Norse tradition, describes Olav as the attacked party, we find both Tyri and Sigrid as "instigators".

The women who in Saxo are made use of for Swein's intentions, in Snorre play independent and important parts. The brain behind the intrigue that leads to Olav's catastrophe in Saxo is Swein Forkbeard, whereas in Snorre it is Sigrid. It is obvious that not ony two conflicting opinions of Olav form the basis of Saxo's and Snorre's different versions, but also divergent opinions of the women involved.

How then is Sigrid described in the two versions? In Snorre we get the impression of a woman with power and authority. Her surname 'the Strong-minded' from the beginning receives its explanation and is later used about her.

Saxo does not mention this surname; nor do we here meet a woman who would deserve it! Saxo frequently says that Sigrid is powerful, but nowhere does he give us that impression. She is exposed to an extraordinarily debasing treatment, which Saxo describes very exhaustively: she is persuaded to go on board Olav's ship, the gang-plank is snatched away and she falls headlong into the water. In this situation she is jeered at for her debauchery, she is the subject of ridicule and taunting. (The Swedes obviously let the queen save herself, although she came very near drowning.) The description of her reaction underlines how ridiculous she appears. Saxo emphasizes how she is taunted and repeats words such as "shame" and "dishonour". He stresses Sigrid's debasement twice by contrasting elevation with disgrace:

– Such an "elevated queen" has been exposed to "the worst disgrace".[9]

– The "majestic and elevated queen" had been brought into a "disgracing" situation and "ridiculed".[10]

Notwithstanding the fact that Saxo does not cherish any great opinion of the Norwegians, he must still be responsible for the detailed description of those infamies to which Sigrid is exposed. It is with ill-concealed delight that Saxo lets Sigrid fall from elevation as deeply as possible into debasement.

In Snorre, however, we meet a proud, independent and self-confident woman. These qualities the author makes very evident: tired of the proposals from the minor kings Sigrid drastically makes an example. She takes Olav's offer kindly but is always on her guard against disrespect, and she becomes incensed when she discovers that the gold ring is fake. (She interprets this as an indication of Olav's treacherous character.) Proudly she rejects his marriage conditions and no less proudly she replies to his insult: "This may well be thy death!" Because of her powerful position she is desirable to Swein Forkbeard. Her power is increased by her eloquence: by finding the proper words she eggs on Swein to fight against her enemy, Olav. Snorre gives us full evidence of a woman who indeed deserves the surname, "the Strong-minded".

Even in other respects than those already mentioned, Saxo and Snorre treat Sigrid in different ways: while Snorre only briefly (in one sentence) mentions "the insult", Saxo bases his whole story on it. In the insult scene Snorre lets Sigrid have the last word and thereby a certain rehabilitation thanks to her reply, "This may well be thy death". In Saxo Sigrid's threat is completely devoid of the force and gravity it exerts in Snorre. Saxo's wording, "she uttered threats of all sorts", hardly implies something calamitous. On the whole Sigrid is allowed to speak herself in Snorre (thanks to his use of direct speech and dialogues), while in Saxo her words are not even related.

The different impressions we get of Sigrid in Saxo and in Snorre are certainly also due to the differences in their narrative technique. Snorre (who represents the Icelandic narrative tradition) does not analyse mental conditions; neither does he give moralizing reflections. Saxo, on the other hand, always commits himself by giving free vent to his own reactions, emotional as well as rational. Where Snorre uses direct speech, Saxo uses indirect,[11] where Snorre lets action speak, Saxo tells us what happens or has happened. By quoting Sigrid *verbatim*, Snorre convinces the reader of her authority. The insult as such makes Sigrid grow in

Snorre, but it makes her shrink piteously in Saxo. Finally it should be emphasized that Snorre does not, even with one word, comment upon either Olav's or Sigrid's reaction, whereas Saxo repeatedly points out the ignominy and shame of the situation.

These two opposing descriptions of Sigrid can only to a small extent be traced to older sources of the battle of Svolder. The explanation why Sigrid is treated so differently by Saxo and Snorre must be sought elsewhere too. The parts allotted to women and the way in which women are described reflect the significance that is attached to them by the author and help to reveal the underlying opinion of women in general. That is where the explanation is to be sought, viz. in the opinion of women, as expressed in each work, Gesta Danorum and Heimskringla:

Heimskringla

Heimskringla's independent and powerful Sigrid is not unique compared with the other women in the work: there are numerous examples of female action and energy:

- We have already seen how Swein's sister Tyri takes her fate into her own hands.
- Gunhild (the widow of Eric Blood-axe), together with her sons, subdues the Orkney Islands and parts of Norway, incites her sons to extend their power, acts as their counsellor and has a great part of the rule in her hand.[12]
- Astrid (the widow of St. Olav) amasses an army, equips her stepson, Magnus the Good, speaks at the *ting* (council) and defends his cause: the recapture of his lost patrimony, Norway.[13]
- And Thora (Sigurd the Crusader's mother) sees to it that a young man, who in her opinion had behaved presumptuously, has his tongue cut off.[14]

It is striking that, on the whole, women play an active and important part: to Snorre it seems quite acceptable and natural that a woman can be a dangerous enemy, and she is allowed to operate on the same footing with men. It should be noticed that Snorre does not seem to find anything remarkable about female independence, will-power and energy. The behaviour and actions of women are mostly depicted without comments: Snorre neither condemns nor praises. Very few women have "bad" qualities attributed to them: one example is Gunhild, who is described as "insidious" and "heartless", and a couple of women are said to be "wanton" (e.g. the goddess Freya). But, as a rule, women are desribed as beautiful and prudent, sometimes good, eloquent or generous. These descriptions, however, give the impression of being stereotypes. Some women are skilled in the witch's art – women seem to have a "natural" relation to magic.

Rolf Heller has shown how all the women in Icelandic Saga are subordinated to certain motifs. In Heimskringla the women often appear in revenge motifs, where they play the parts of inciters. We have already met with Tyri and Sigrid, who instigate revenge. We also find several examples of discontented wives who kill or try to kill their husbands – or in other ways cause their deaths.[15]

To sum up: women play an important role in Snorre's history. In Heimskringla at least 150 women are given names; more than half only incidentally, it is true, but there still remain a considerable number of women on whom a closer attention has been bestowed.

The fact that so many women are endowed with names is due to the way the Saga presents its persons: the genealogy is carefully recorded and even the women of the families are included in these enumerations. Whether the significance which is attached to the distaff side has any particular meaning or not is difficult to know, especially as the Sagas to a great extent deal with well-known and class-conscious families.

As to the characterization of women there are many things that remind one of the "virago-ideal" of late classical antiquity: women often have "male" qualities attributed to them. Even the early medieval ideal of women as her husband's counsellor can be traced in Snorre, but he does not seem to share the worries about female indecency that are typical of certain medieval writers. Nor do we notice much of the ascetic ideal of the Church or its explicit denigration of women. If *vita contemplativa* was more highly valued than *vita activa* in earlier medieval times, the opposite seems to be true of women in Heimskringla.

Even if these women are subordinated to various motifs, they are allowed, within these limits, to be active, and they are sometimes described as being equal to men. We do not meet the depreciating view of women that distinguishes so much of contemporary European literature, at least not in the same guise. The question is, however, whether woman as "instigator", "dangerous enemy" and "sourceress" should be connected with the clerical image of women as a menace and a danger to man.

Gesta Danorum

While in Snorre Sigrid is one of many powerful women who inspire respect and play historically important roles, in Saxo she is one of many powerless and unimportant women who do not act themselves, but are subjected to the actions of other people, mainly men. And their role is frequently far from glorious: in Gesta Danorum we meet a whole string of other queens, who, like Sigrid, are exposed to degrading treatment and have their honour tarnished:

1. Queen Gerutha is subjected to Amleth's wrath, scorn and contempt. In the severe lecture he delivers she is compared to a mare in heat.[16]
2. The low birth of the British queen is revealed by Amleth in a painful way. Because of her unworthy behaviour (which Saxo carefully describes) Amleth concludes that she is a bondmaid.[17]
3. Queen Hanunde's unfaithfulness is revealed – also in a painful way – by Eric ("the Shrewd-spoken"). She is later repudiated by King Frode.[18]
4. Ingeld's German-born queen also gets into trouble: on two occasions the warrior, Starkad, throws her gifts to him right into her face (Saxo seems to have repeated the same scene twice!) and delivers a most severe lecture, in which the queen is blamed for her love of luxury and the introduction of foreign – German – manners, luxury and gluttony.[19]
5. Even Siger's queen has her gift rejected, when Hagbard flings the drinking-cup that she has scornfully offered him directly at her head, "so that he drenched her face with the sprinkled wine".[20]
6. Still worse is the misfortune that the Slavic queen meets with. Unsuspecting she is pierced with a sword by her prisoners, when she puts her head through a doorway out of curiosity. Before she dies, Saxo lets her, like Sigrid, utter various – empty – threats. (As Saxo puts it: "A flood of ... threats against her slayer poured from her dying lips").[21]
7. Jarmerik's queen Swanhild is exposed to the most degrading and cruel treatment. Wrongfully accused of unfaithfulness and incest she is condemned to be trampled to death by horses. The refusal of the animals to touch her is explained by her beauty, which is said to have bewitched them. Therefore the queen is turned with her face to the ground. The punishment can now be executed, and Saxo coldly states: "Such was the end of Swanhild."[22]

Common to all these queens, Sigrid included, is that they are subordinate characters, whom we meet only in these dishonouring and ignominious situations. They do not play their parts actively, but merely as the butts of degrading speech and debasing treatment. Saxo often remains indifferent to their fates: not even Swanhild's tragic and horrible fate has induced him to show compassion. Instead, a malicious joy is sometimes discernible.

In the last books of the work there are also queens who are recorded in a far from glorious way:

Eric the Lamb's German-born queen, Liutgard,[23] is named only to be criticized and so is Swein Grade's similarly German-born queen, although Saxo here only reports a bad rumour and then refutes it.[24]

Valdemar's queen, Sophia, receives all the blame for foolish marriage contracts with the Emperor,[25] and Kanute's German-born queen, Gerthruda, becomes historical because on one occasion she cries out of "female fright".[26] (Her fright seems indeed justifiable, since she sees that Valdemar's life is threatened. Although it is obviously her crying that averts the danger, Saxo does not thank her, but the Lord.)

With these examples I will not maintain that Saxo's attitude towards these women should be explained by some special antipathy for queens, even if his hateful attitude towards those of German origin could be a reaction from his dislike and fear of German influence, so often discernible in Gesta Danorum! In Saxo's own time this influence was expanding, owing to Kanute's marriage to Gerthruda, the daughter of Henry "the Lion". But since Gesta Danorum mostly deals with members of the royal families, it is not mainly as queens that we should view these women, but as representatives of the female sex. Not only queens are debased in different ways:

1. Hjalte's harlot has her nose cut off, when she is impudent enough to bring up the question of his successor as a lover.[27]
2. Gotwar is stoned to death because of her complicity in concealing a crime.[28]
3. The princess Helga's relationship with the lewd goldsmith is described in distasteful detail, and, caught in the act by Starkad, Helga is blamed for lacking honour and chastity.[29]
4. The princess Rinda, who is cheated into taking Odin into her service – he is disguised as a woman – is exposed to his indiscreet advances (described in detail). When she turns ill (owing to Odin's magic), she is

tied to her bed to be "treated" and "healed" by Odin, the false maiden. It is true that this rape arouses Saxo's loathing; he is upset about
Odin's acting, but he willingly dwells upon it – even on its details.[30]
Debasement as such obviously seems to have appealed to Saxo; if the
women are of high station, their "fall" is the greater. But common to
most women in the examples given is that they get into trouble or are
criticized because of their faults and deficiencies (and thus justly, from
Saxo's point of view.)

Characteristic of Saxo is that he constantly confronts female weakness
with male strength, female fright with male courage and female viciousness with male virtue. This opposition pervades Saxo's whole work,
stamps the division of roles and permeates characterizations and language. In contrast with Snorre, Saxo does not make a secret of his opinion of
women: not only does it appear indirectly, it is also clearly and distinctly
formulated, with the greatest emphasis after the episode where Hermutruda (another queen!) in spite of her vow of fidelity has failed and
embraces Amleth's slayer.[31] Saxo's comment on her behaviour expands
to a sharp attack on women in general:

> "Thus all vows of woman are loosed by change of fortune and
> melted by the shifting of time; the faith of their soul rests on a
> slippery foothold and is weakened by casual changes; glib in promi-
> ses, and as sluggish in performance, all manner of lustful promptings
> enslave it, and it bounds away with panting and precipitate desire,
> forgetful of old things in the ever hot pursuit after something
> fresh."[32]

What Saxo here says about woman is abundantly illustrated in Gesta
Danorum, in episodes that are real *exempla* of woman's weaknesses,
vices and general unreliability. We meet women who are lured by different desires, women who have weaknesses for beautiful words or charming faces. Some women are cunning, some are covetous of power,
splendour and honour. Several of the queens mentioned are just such
exempla:
1. Gerutha is punished for her faithlessness and wantonness.
2. Hanunde is gullible and weak and is punished because of her faithlessness.
3. Ingeld's queen is haughty, fickle, false and loves sensuous enjoyments.

4. Siger's queen is scornful and presumptuous.

5. The Slavic queen tries to dominate the men.

– As for Swanhild, her fate rather illustrates Jarmerik's cruelty and his counsellor's evil than female faithlessness – Saxo actually mentions her innocence. Here the very contrast between beauty and crudity seems to have fascinated Saxo – but he does not care at all for Swanhild's person.

6. Queen Liutgard's honour and decency did not rank as high as her birth, Saxo writes.

7. The bad rumour about Swein Grade's queen said that she had introduced German, effeminating habits.

8. Queen Sophia is criticized for he ambitiousness, and

9. Queen Gerthruda illustrates female weakness.

Examples of female faults and deficiencies are found everywhere in Gesta Danorum, but especially in that part which deals with heathen times, i.e. the first nine books. Still, Saxo praises ancient women for their chastity, shyness, decency and honour. – This surprising appraisal, then, must be understood as an implicit criticism of contemporary women – and morals – and as an expression of the woman-ideal, for which Saxo is pleading. This ideal can be traced in several places in the work and has much in common with the woman-ideal of the Church. Among those few women who gain distinction in Saxo, the chaste and shy ones are especially noticeable, as well as those who sacrifice themselves – to the point of complete self-destruction:

Bodil, Eric Egode's queen, is said to be a splendid example of female patience; she resigns herself to her husband's open intercourse with concubines, and even adorns them and is good to them. So great is her wish to please her husband that she allows other women to charm him, knowing that she herself could not do it.[33]

The ideal woman exists for her husband's sake and on his conditions; this is a thought that frequently occurs. We have seen how Hjalte reacted when he understood that he was dispensable. Saxo shares his indignation, and the girl's punishment is described as just.

Gunhild, the Swedish King Asmund's queen, gains distinction when she commits suicide to be spared from surviving her husband. (Moreover, this is the only thing that is told about her.) By doing this, "she shares his grave with greater honour than, when alive, she shared his bed", Saxo thinks.[34] To Saxo it is quite right that a woman should follow

her husband to death – not only does Gunhild do this but also the vigorous Swanhwid[35] and the faithful Signe.[36] But women who to this end
take their own lives are praiseworthy, since they have raised themselves
above their sisters, who by their nature are weak, frightened and unfaith-
ful. – Hermutruda's deceit towards Amleth verifies this.

In spite of his low opinion of women in general, Saxo could not deny
the presence of strong, resolute and independently-acting women; such
women existed in the tradition upon which he built, as well as in his own
time. On the other hand, he could insert them into his history on his own
conditions, and these had probably been determined by suspiciousness
and dislike of powerful women. Those who are not denigrated (because
of their malice and wickedness) are disparaged in other ways. Since
denigration is easy to recognize, I will, instead, draw attention to other
kinds of disparagement by giving some examples of women upon whom
suspicion is cast or whose importance and achievements are "reduced":

1. Urse, Rolf Krake's mother – and sister – discovers that Athisl has
   married her in order to make use of the kinship to relax the tribute.
   She takes revenge by escaping with her husband's treasures. Since
   Athisl indeed does not enlist Saxo's sympathies, one expects Urse's
   action to gain Saxo's approval. But her deception of her husband
   primarily illustrates the faithlessness and untrustworthiness of women.
   And furthermore: Saxo casts suspicion upon her and reports a rumour,
   saying that Urse herself had seized the treasure, a rumour he is inclined to trust.[37]

2. Gurid, the only surviving member of the Danish royal family, saves
   the kingdom from extinction by producing a son (Harald Hildetand),
   whose life she later saves. The merit of the birth is, however, not
   ascribed to her but to the warrior, Haldan, who in spite of various
   obstacles resolutely marries her. She had e.g. made vow of chastity,
   which was not very praiseworthy with regard to the situation of the
   kingdom. In the battle, in which Haldan later tries to unite the split
   country, Gurid appears disguised as a man and saves her son by carrying him away from the turmoil. But as Harald then gets an arrow in his
   buttocks, his mother's help brought him more shame than good, Saxo
   states.[38]

3. Hede is a woman warrior, who fights bravely on Harald's side in the
   battle of Bråvalla. When the victor, the Swedish King Ring, divides
   the Danish kingdom, Hede is set by him to rule Zealand and Jutland.

In Saxo's description Denmark now has reached its nadir: the kingdom is split and ruled by a queen! To the Zealanders it seemed a shame to be subjected to a woman. Therefore they asked for assistance against her. Hede's importance and strength is considerably reduced, since she is made to abstain from her power by means of a mere threat – and not real fighting.[39]

4. Thyre Danebod ("Danicae maiestatis caput") has been given a prominent position in Gesta Danorum. Among other things Saxo mentions that it was she who started to build the wall against Germany, "Danevirke", an accomplishment Saxo gives her credit for. But he hastens to mention those who deserve the real merit, namely Valdemar and Absalon. Saxo writes: "they finished with male genius the unfinished endeavours of that brave woman, working the more efficiently as they knew themselves to be superior to women in strength."[40]

5. Ladgerda bravely helps Ragnar in a fight but exposes him to danger of death when he comes to woo her. Since Ragnar survives, they marry(!), but Ragnar can not forget her deceit and therefore soon repudiates her. Ladgerda's second husband meets with a greater misfortune than Ragnar: he is killed by his wife. Saxo writes: "the presumptuous and self-indulgent woman would rather rule without her husband than share the glory with him.[41]

6. The Norwegian queen Gunhild is mentioned only once in Gesta Danorum. She is said to have made a spear hover in the air and hit her son's slayer – all by witch-craft. This is the only thing Saxo tells us about one of the truly leading actors of Heimskringla – Eric Blood-axe's powerful widow![42]

7. The women warriors form a distinct group in Gesta Danorum. Saxo seems to be impressed by their "souls of men" in "bodies of women" but he is eager to stress that they are all finally defeated, most of them easily. Harald Hildetand, who defeated three women warriors, did it "with unarmed breast" as Saxo points out. They are never allowed to be a serious threat to men – at least not to Danish men! (cf. Hede)[43]

Least exposed to disparagement – even if traces of "reduction" can be noticed – are those women who have been of use to men, e.g. Swanhwid[44] and Gunwar,[45] i.e. women who have subordinated their strength or prudence to the needs of men. Most exposed are those independently-acting women, who do not subordinate themselves to anything else than their own will. It is to this "group" that Sigrid belongs, the woman who in

Snorre causes war between neighbour nations, but in Saxo is devoid of
every influence and thus has been "reduced" to unimportance – beyond
recognition!

Conclusions

Jørgen Olrik, one of the few scholars who have commented at all on
Saxo's female figures, stated that the descriptions of women in the "saga-
part" primarily reflected "the strong-willed woman-ideal of the heathen
heroic literature".[46] – From Saxo's way of describing strong-willed and
active women the conclusion, however, can be drawn that these women
did not correspond to the ideal that he embraced or was commissioned to
favour, an ideal that, instead, reminds us of the ideal we find in the
edifying literature of the Church. It is true that this strong-willed woman-
ideal is reflected in both Heimskringla and Gesta Danorum, but in very
different ways. Why?

My answer is that the mirror which Saxo holds up gives a distorted
picture; it diminishes and distorts where it is not a downright laughing-
mirror. There are of course several reasons why the images of women
differ as much as they do. In my thesis I am at pains to try to give an
exposition of them. Here I can only suggest where the causes are to be
found:

In Saxo the influence of contemporary European literature, clerical as
well as profane, is more noticeable than in Snorre. Due attention must be
paid to the various aims of Gesta Danorum itself, moral, political, clerical, church-political and juridical, since the role of woman (like the role
of man) is naturally subordinated to these aims. Attention must also be
paid to the various motifs; I consider it very important not to isolate the
female figures from the context! And, further, I consider it misleading –
and anachronistic – to believe that Saxo, whenever he is describing a
woman, in the first place intends to give a portrait of *her* personality; the
women have many functions in Gesta Danorum, and one of the most
important is to illustrate the personal qualities of *the men* involved! (This
is often done by means of contrasting effects, e.g. if a man is weak, we
often find that the woman is strong – and vice versa!)

In Gesta Danorum, Common Weal is the guiding star, and as the
individuals must subordinate themselves to the demands of Society, woman must be subordinated to man – or else she constitutes a menace to
man – and consequently to the established order of Society. It is the

unbridled will, as well as the viciousness and the emasculating influence in general, that make woman so dangerous: not only does she threaten man's military ability but also his virtue – and salvation.

A concept in court rhetoric is *detrectatio,* i.e. "belittlement" of the opponent. As a menace to man and Society, woman is to be considered an opponent or enemy, and as such she is systematically belittled by Saxo before contemporary and future judges. I will sum up the ways in which this *detrectatio* finds its expression:

1. In proportion to men only little room is made for women in the history. This, however, cannot be laid only to Saxo's charge; this kind of disparagement has been used by all historians even into our own time. Women are often allotted a passive role, and most of them remain nameless. (It has obviously not been considered worth-while to record their names.) This strengthens the impression of their unimportance.
2. Even active women are described as subjected to the actions of men. We seldom meet them in action, and their actions are often faded out or are passed over in silence.
3. Many women are exposed to debasing treatment, at which their dignity and reputation are lost or seriously tarnished.
4. In the parts which are assigned to them, women often illustrate Evil, Vice or Weakness. Some women are denigrated, others, whose influence or achievements can be of a positive kind, have their importance more or less "reduced".
5. What Saxo does not achieve by these methods he achieves by means of comments and criticism – direct or indirect. In several cases he is very outspoken in criticizing women, in some cases he reports rumours in order to cast suspicion upon them.

In spite of his obvious misogyny and all his talk about female weakness, we understand that Saxo took women seriously. If Snorre admitted that woman could be a dangerous enemy, this, to a still greater extent, applies for Saxo: this appears from his consistent endeavour to try to render her harmless.

Most of the women in Gesta Danorum are more or less passive: there are comparatively few women who really act. The active women are generally to be found in the heathen part, i.e. the fist nine books. Here we can find women who conjure and tell fortunes, make war and kill, plan or execute reprisals. But the activity that is exercised by the few active women in the second, "Christian" part of the work is quite different. Their activity is e.g. confined to warnings and advice, gifts to the Church – and instead of vengeance – empty threats. The colourless and shadowy women in the Christian part of Gesta Danorum present a striking contrast to the colourful women in the heathen section, where they sometimes even put the men in the shade.

With book 10 women almost completely cease to intervene actively and independently. Sigrid's "fall" in this book from power and elevation down to powerlessness and humiliation therefore illustrates not only the vicissitudes of fortune or the notorious barbarism of Norwegians (two frequent motifs in Saxo), but also the fate of the female characters in Gesta Danorum: in the heathen part they play historically important parts, but thereafter their influence is insignificant. However, the influence that women exert in heathen times is often of a negative kind: they then represent the power of Evil. And as exercisers of magic, the tools of Evil, we meet comparatively more women than men.

I should like to make a reference to Kurt Johannesson[47] and what he has pointed out as Gesta Danorum's basic theme, namely the struggle between Chaos and Logos, i.e. the female and the male principles in Platonic Cosmology. It is in the first nine books that we meet the efforts of the constantly faithless female Matter to overthrow the cosmic system. With the introduction of Christian faith the power of Matter is broken – and from the 9th book the magic, too, fades away as well as the fatalism. Against this background it is interesting to see how female power, like material power, in Gesta Danorum belongs to ancient times and then helps to illustrate "the imperfect way of the heathen man to master his world".[48]

However the differences between the first nine and the last seven books should be explained, it remains a fact that one of the teachings that Saxo gives us runs as follows: Activity among women is unnatural and often dangerous; it mainly belongs to bygone – heathen – times.

II. THYRE DANEBOD IN GESTA DANORUM

Introduction

The story about Thyre Danebod[49] contains one of the most complicated descriptions of women in Saxo, apparently full of obscurities and contradictions. Saxo emphasizes her prudence and wits, but also her shrewdness and art of dissimulation. She appears to be both extremely purposeful and self-asserting, *and* submissive and self-sacrificing. She, who by her father – and by Saxo himself – is considered to be unsuitable to govern a kingdom (England), becomes the saviour of Denmark because of her clever and brave policy of defence and recapture. When Thyre's father makes her sons his heirs, Saxo writes:[50]

"Nor was he unwise; for he knew that it beseemed men to enjoy the sovereignty rather than women, and considered that he ought to separate the lot of his unwarlike daughter from that of her valiant sons."

But with his story about Thyre Saxo gives us an example of the contrary: the men in this episode prove to be extremely unfit for leading a people; instead it is the woman, Thyre, who with power and authority assumes the leader's part. How is the complicated picture of Thyre in Saxo to be explained? Has Saxo had any intention of making a portrait of Thyre? The pieces of information about her are spread among three different places in Gesta Danorum, in the ninth and tenth books. Her functions in the different contexts are probably subordinated to different purposes, which have determined Saxo's treatment of her. To begin with I shall summarize Saxo's "story":

Thyre according to Saxo

Book 9, pp. 266-268: When king Gorm was counselled by the elders to be married, he proposed to Thyre, the daughter of Æthelred, the king of the English. Saxo writes:

"She surpassed other women in seriousness and energy, and laid the condition on her suitor that she would not marry him till she had received Denmark as a morning-gift."[51]

This was agreed upon and she was betrothed to Gorm. But on the first night that she came into the marriage-bed, she asked her husband most earnestly that she should be allowed to go free from intercourse with him for three days. For she had decided not to be embraced till she had learnt by some omen in a dream that their marriage would be blessed with children. Saxo tells us therefore that to this end she pretended to be chaste and shy. (Saxo also tells us about another explanation, which he, however, does not believe: "Others suppose she declined the caresses of the nuptial couch so that by her abstinence she could win her bridegroom over to Christianity.")[52] Gorm respected Thyre's wish, "believing that her prayers, which really sprang from calculation, were allied to her chastity,"[53] and Saxo particularly points out his chivalrousness as something remarkable. Then, in his dreams, Gorm had a vision, which by Thyre was interpreted as implying that she would be blessed with offspring. Now she "gave her husband the welcome chance to possess her,"[54] telling him that she would not have fulfilled their marriage at all, if she had not received this omen of her being fruitful. Fate did not disappoint her hopes: soon she was the fortunate mother of two sons, who were given the names of Kanute and Harald. When the boys had grown up they put out a fleet and attacked their neighbours, even England, where their grandfather was so impressed by their spirit and violence that he passed over his daughter and bequeathed England to them in his will. But Thyre, who saw her sons inheriting her father's property, did not complain of being disinherited herself, Saxo says, for she thought that this preference over herself was honourable to her, rather than insulting.

So great was Gorm's love for his elder son that he had sworn he would slay with his own hand whoever first brought him news of his death. When, Thyre, therefore, heard sure tidings that Kanute had perished in Ireland, nobody dared to tell Gorm. Then Thyre fell back on her cunning to defend her: she dressed the old king in filthy garments and brought him other signs of grief as well. When he asked if it was Kanute's death she declared, she answered that it was rather he himself who did it. By her answer she made her husband a dead man and herself a widow, Saxo writes, regretting her misfortune.

Book 10, pp. 269-272: Kanute's brother, Harald, who succeeded Gorm, differed from his father in at least trying to enlarge his supremacy and his riches, which, however, he only partly managed to do. England was lost, but in Vendland Harald founded a Viking kingdom with Julin (Jomsborg) as the capital. A war against Sweden he had to interrupt hastily, because without resistance the Emperor had invaded Denmark, which "lacked royal leadership".[55] Harald hastened to the defence of his country, but the Emperor had already reached the "Limfjord", before Harald drove him back. Now Thyre wanted to save the country from attacks from abroad and therefore started to build a wall with a moat across Jylland between Slesvig and the western sea. "The brave woman's imperfect plan"[56] was completed by Valdemar and Absalon, Saxo tells us, pointing out that their work was the more glorious in that they knew themselves superior to female energy. But Saxo also informs us that she freed Scania from Sweden and the heavy tribute, "as she had male courage in her female body. Thus she drove back the enemy partly by the moat and the wall, partly by weapons, and protected as firmly and safely all the borders of the country."[57]

P. 274: When Thyre died, her son Harald gave her a magnificent funeral and buried her near his father's grave-mound. Thyre's death caused general mourning: it was believed that her death had put an end to the welfare of the country.

Saxo thus lets us meet a woman who presents her suitor with a most remarkable condition before accepting his proposal, and who then makes him agree to sexual abstinence in order to gain an omen of offspring. She rejoices in her father's decision to make her sons his heirs, she brings her husband death and finally she successfully takes over the defence of Denmark and appears as the rescuer of her country, for which she gains distinction in Saxo.

Does Saxo's information about Thyre have any historical foundation?

The Jellinge stone and the different traditions about Thyre

What can be stated about Thyre with certainty is confined to the words on the smaller Jellinge stone, the stone which Gorm erected over his wife: "King Gorm made this barrow over Thyre, his wife, *Denmark's healer*" (=*Tanmarkar but*). The surname, *tanmarkarbut,* was later inseparably connected with Thyre,[58] but the explanations of this name, which come from the end of the 12th century, are different:

In Icelandic literature the deed which is ascribed to Thyre is related to her capacity to interpret dreams. In the Jomsvikinga- and Olav Tryggvasonsagas Gorm dreams that he sees three white, later three red and at last three black cows rise from the sea and go ashore. Thyre takes the dream to mean that three times three years' misfortune will come upon Denmark. Therefore, for several summers on end, she has barley and other products collected to be distributed among her subjects and thereby she succeeds in averting famine. For this reason she gets her surname.

In Sven Aggesen and Saxo, however, her contributions are related to the border: Thyre builds "Danevirke" and therefore in Sven is given the surname *Decus Datiae,* in Saxo *Danicae maiestatis caput,* according to *L. Weibull* both of them "principally free transpositions of tanmarkarbut".[59]

The differences between these explanations raised L. Weibull's suspicion that it was the surname that had generated the stories of her deeds and not vice versa.[60] L. Weibull showed that the Icelandic story about the famine, which is based on Genesis 41 (where Joseph averts the famine in Egypt) was historically useless. How, then, should the Danish tradition about Thyre as the builder of "Danevirke" be explained? – This also was discarded by L. Weibull as historically useless:[61] "Danevirke" had already been mentioned in Franconian annals under the year 808 as built by Godfred, king of the Danes, i.e. more than a century before Thyre's lifetime and three and a half centuries before the first statements about Thyre as its builder.[62]

How have these different traditions originated? – L. Weibull answers:[63]

"On the stone in Jellinge is written: Tanmarkarbut. It must be taken for granted that the last word means 'remedy', 'improvement', as it still does today. But the words on the stone did not give information about the deed that had created such a surname. In Iceland the healing of the country in the case of averting famine originated from the surname in connection with the story of Joseph. Here imagination was given free scope. In Denmark too it was an interpretation of her surname which inspired the story. Here the learned historians were the inventors. They split up the surname etymologically. 'Mark means border in Danish' – marck lingua danica terminus est – Robert of Ely says in Knut Lavard's biography a generation before Sven Ågesen. This interpretation gave the starting-point, and with this the way to the border lay open. Tanmarkar, which on the stone must mean Denmark('s), was interpreted as 'the Danish border', 'the border of the Danes', by learned men. When this was combined with the other word of the surname, 'bod' ("healing"), they could present Thyre as 'the healer of the Danish border'. But Denmark's especial border was at that time the southern border against Germany with its wall. Thyre improved this border. The wall became Tyre's work."

In accordance with *H. Brix,* L. Weibull thought the surname *tanmarkarbut* was to be related to Gorm and not to Thyre. As far as he is concerned Thyre has "disappeared from the historical saga".[64]

It is obvious that Thyre's historical authencity is very weak. An interesting point here is, however, that in the 12th century there was a strong tradition about her greatness and importance to Denmark.

By Sven Aggesen's and Saxo's time obviously so little was known about this Thyre that the authors were free to concoct their own stories. Neither Sven Aggesen nor Saxo were presumably familiar with the smaller Jellinge stone, according to which Gorm had buried his wife: in Saxo, Thyre's barrow had been raised by Harald, in Sven, both Gorm's and Thyre's barrows were due to him.[65] It is in Sven Aggesen that we first meet the picture of Thyre as the builder of "Danevirke":[66]

Thyre according to Sven

Gorm's wife Thyre was a woman to whom Sven attributes all kinds of praiseworthy qualities. She was beautiful, chaste and wise: "One would think that from a well she had drawn Nestor's prudence, Odysseus's shrewdness and Solomon's wisdom".[67] At this time the Emperor (Otto) had made Denmark tributary, according to Sven a consequence of king Gorm's laziness and weakness. In the Emperor there arose a desire to entice the chaste queen. He sent his messengers to Thyre under the pretence of demanding payment of the tribute, but their real mission was to persuade her how much more appropriate it would be if she – with her beauty and wisdom – were Empress instead of the queen of a tributary country. Thyre asked for time to consider. She devised an ingenious stratagem, and when the messengers came back, she explained that she was ready to do as the Emperor wanted. But at the same time she pointed out how hazardous it was for her to abandon her husband and marry another: in order to protect herself from blame, she would have to buy herself free by means of a big sum, and therefore she demanded that three years' tribute be allotted to her. The Emperor willingly agreed but claimed hostages as security. Now the queen sent word all over the country that everybody should gather at Slesvig and build a huge wall. When the Emperor head of this, he sent his messengers to Thyre to receive an explanation. Thyre cleverly managed to explain it all away. After the three years were gone, the fortification was ready, and when a picked army from the Emperor came to fetch Thyre, she could proudly answer:

"What the Emperor demands and claims, I decline, what he desires, I shun ... I will at once free the tributary Danes from the yoke of slavery and never more honour or submit to you."[68]

The Emperor's men had to return home empty-handed. It is true that the hostages the Emperor had seized were killed, but "with the death of these few men" Thyre had redeemed a whole country, writes Sven Aggesen.[69]

Sven Aggesen places Thyre in a purely invented historical context, full of adventurous motifs and with features from Vergil and Justin, as well as from German history.[70]

Saxo – like the Icelanders – speaks about Thyre's capacity to interpret dreams but places it in a new context. He makes Thyre an English princess, thereby borrowing features from the Anglo-Saxon Æthelfled's history. This Æthelfled was said to have built several fortifications along the border between Danish and Anglo-Saxon areas in England. Like Æthelfled in Henry of Huntingdon, Thyre in Saxo becomes a daughter of king Æthelred.[71]

In the Icelandic literature, where the border motif is lacking, Gorm definitely plays the dominant role; in the Danish literature, where we find the border motif and "Danevirke", Thyre plays the leading part. In both Sven Aggesen and Saxo Gorm is a weak and powerless king.[72] But the differences between Sven's and Saxo's Thyre-stories are many and striking. Still, L. Weibull writes about Saxo and his relation to Sven (my italics):[73]

"His whole story is just *a paraphrase of his predecessor's with an addition* about the newly-built church in Jellinge and *the corrections* which his statement about Gorm's death before Thyre demanded."

The question is, however, whether Saxo's story is not a great deal more than a "paraphrase" with "additions" and "corrections": on closer inspection it appears to be written in conscious opposition to that of Sven Aggesen; while Sven exalts her to the skies and unreservedly gives her the whole merit of having rescued the country, Saxo is less obtrusive and provides his picture of Thyre with several important reservations.

Saxo's description of Thyre. Analysis

In Sven Aggesen it is only the southern border of Denmark that Thyre defends; in Saxo it is also the border between Denmark and Sweden. But at the same time as Saxo "augments" her greatness, he reduces it: Saxo needs Thyre's greatness for his own purposes: he is critical towards both Gorm and Harald. Gorm did nothing to enlarge his power, and Harald neglected Denmark, building up his position of power in Vendland and helping Styrbjörn to regain his power in Sweden, thereby leaving Denmark open for the Emperor's attacks. Instead, it was Thyre who, thanks to her wise policy, succeeded not only in recapturing Scania from Sweden but also in defending the country against attacks from the south. Thyre's contributions to Denmark form an effective contrast to Gorm's lack of enterprise and Harald's lack of judgment; her greatness and power illustrate Gorm's and Harald's unimportance and weakness.

But in Saxo there is nothing of Sven Aggesen's story about the Emperor's proposal and Thyre's cunning tactics of procrastination. The key role, which Sven Aggesen from the beginning gives Thyre in the defence against the Emperor, she has partly lost in Saxo: he reduces her achievements by letting Harald return home at last to drive the Germans back. It is true that Saxo mentions that Thyre started to build the wall against Germany, but he immediately hastens to point out that it is not she but Valdemar and Absalon who have the real merit: those were the ones who finished the work:[74]

"They finished with male genius the unfinished work of the brave woman, achieving a much more excellent work as they knew themselves to be superior to female energy."

Saxo also gives a different picture of Thyre's *person* from Sven Aggesen: Sven had emphasized and praised Thyre's beauty and chastity. In Saxo we hear nothing at all about her looks, and the chastity she displays is repeatedly said to be only pretended:[75]

"Thus, *under pretence of self-control*, she deferred her experience of marriage, and *veiled under a show of modesty* her wish to learn her issue. She put off lustful intercourse, inquiring, *under the feint of chastity*, into the fortune she would have in continuing her line."

Not only does Saxo accentuate explicitly that her chastity is not real; he also makes it appear by Thyre's own way of acting: as soon as she knew for certain that she would be blessed with offspring, she

"discarded the idea of putting off the consummation, eagerly renounced the virginity she had implored him to preserve and, exchanging celibacy for sexual love, gave her husband the welcome chance to possess her."[76]

Saxo clearly states that Thyre's entreaty for abstinence originated in a wish first to receive an omen about offspring and not in chastity. Now the question arises:

1. Why did she pretend to be chaste? – Saxo actually hints at the answer (after the description of Gorm's dream):[77] »By a scheme as subtle as it was strange her simulated shyness developed into a knowledge that she was to bear children".

Thyre thus has a plan. What plan? To this question there are no direct answers in Saxo's text, but still he gives us certain clues, which indicate that Thyre from the very beginning wanted to secure power in Denmark:

To accept Gorm's proposal Thyre demanded *Denmark as a morning-gift*. This extraordinary demand is not even commented upon by Saxo! Not only is this the sole time he mentions the custom of such gifts, but the demand is furthermore so unexampled that his silence appears to be suspect. Byt letting Gorm immediately accept her demand Saxo more than evidently illustrates how badly this king administered his kingdom.

2. What, then, did Gorm's promise to give Thyre Denmark as a morning-gift imply? – Since Saxo leaves us in the lurch by observing complete silence we have to consult other sources dealing with the usage of morning-gifts. Unfortunately one looks in vain for regulations concerning this in the Danish provincial laws.[78] We know from folk-ballads that the usage was known in Denmark during ancient times, but in order to get more detailed information we must turn to Swedish law, which is supposed to have influenced the Danish in this respect.[79] According to Swedish law the morning-gift did not go to the wife until the husband was dead.[80] And in the provincial laws the following is prescribed: if there were no children in the marriage, the morning-gift went to the one of the pair who outlived the other, and if there were children, the morning-gift was reckoned as their inheritance through their mother.[81]

Provided that it is these regulations that the reader of Gesta Danorum is to have in mind, Thyre's actions are fully understandable: Thyre had demanded – and obtained – Denmark as her morning-gift, and naturally she wanted to be sure of giving birth to heirs: if she died before Gorm, Denmark then was to go not to Gorm but to her children. And if Gorm died before her, she herself could gain dominion over all Denmark. But she could probably not expect to be allowed to remain in undisturbed possession, as the possession comprised a whole kingdom – if she had no children at her side to defend their maternal inheritance! Thus certainty about grown-up children was very important for Thyre's plans concerning Denmark.

3. How was she to find out for certain that the marriage with Gorm would be blessed with issue? – According to magical ideas the dreams of the first bridal nights were considered especially important: if sexual abstinence was observed during these nights, it was more likely that the dreams would hold good.[82] And the Church recommended abstinence during these nights (so-called Tobias nights) on different grounds: according to certain collections of decrees, sexual abstinence during these nights would guarantee that the children who were then born were certainly legitimate and lawful heirs before God and men.[83]

But in order not to arouse Gorm's suspicions Thyre had to conceal her real purposes behind the abstinence. Instead, she pretended to be chaste in order to have her will – to avoid sexual intercourse. And she is favoured by Fortune: the gullible Gorm, who believes in her chastity and – to Saxo's astonishment – respects her wish, has strange visions in his dreams:[84]

"He imagined that two birds, one larger than the other, fluttered forth out of his wife's womb, then hovered in the air before soaring to the sky and after a short interval returned to perch one on each of his hands. A second and a third time, after refreshing themselves in short rest, they took off with outstretched wings, till at last the smaller of them flew back alone, its feathers smeared with blood. Bewildered by the vision, still deep in slumber he emitted a groan prompted by his stupefaction and then filled the house with rousing cries."

Far from being hesitant because of the disappearance of one of the birds, the bloodsmeared wings of the other and Gorm's "rousing cries", Thyre, instead, is very eager to fulfil the marriage. She interprets the dream as a sure presage of grown-up children. (Has she perhaps even a presentiment of Gorm's future misfortune?) How, then, does Thyre explain to Gorm that she has now abandoned her wish to maintain abstinence?

As the chaste woman she pretends to be, she refers to the certainty of her fertility,[85] which she had inferred from the images in his dream; for a chaste woman married life (i.e. sexual intercourse) could be defended only for purposes of procreation. In this way Thyre succeeds in concealing what kind of certainty she wanted and why she wanted it.

Then Saxo – in his turn – conceals the real reason why she saw her father make her sons his heirs without envy. He describes it as if Thyre is passed over, but in reality it is not Thyre but her brother who has been passed over (which Saxo tells us in another context in Book 10). The fact that she rejoiced in her father's decision is quite natural: now she could be sure of power and influence in her home country as well as in Denmark.

From the beginning Thyre is not interested in Gorm but in the opportunity of obtaining the power that the marriage to him could give her. It turns out to be one of her sons who finally provides her with this opportunity to seize the power herself:

4. Gorm loved his eldest son so much that he had sworn to slay with his own hands whoever first brought him news about his death. No one except Thyre dared to undertake this task, Saxo tells us. The explanation probably is that Thyre now saw an opportunity of obtaining a "cause of widowhood", as Saxo so insinuatingly puts it (after Gorm's death).[86] By taking the royal robes off her aged husband and dressing him in filthy garments, bringing him other signs of grief as well, she makes Gorm finally burst out: "Do you declare to me the death of Kanute?" – Owing to her answer: "That is proclaimed by your presage, not by mine", she impels Gorm to punish himself with death – true to his own oath.[87]

Now Thyre has reached her goal: Denmark has passed to her: she now has supreme power in Denmark and at her side she has the younger son Harald, the lawful heir.

Conclusion

Thyre Danebod, as she appears in Gesta Danorum, is Saxo's own creation, based on the only thing that was known about her: that she was Denmark's "healer". Out of this "fact" Sven Aggesen had made his whole fanciful story about Thyre: here she became historical exclusively because of her wise politics of defence. But in Saxo this is not what is pointed out: here her role as Denmark's real ruler is touched upon quite cursorily. On the other hand her role as a fiancée, bride, wife, widow and mother is treated in detail with the result that we get the image of a woman who surely and purposefully builds up a position of power for herself and her children. What Saxo emphasizes is her effort to make Denmark, i.e. the royal power, inheritable.

In the first sentence of the 10th book Saxo speaks about Harald's "hereditary supremacy".[88] It was his mother he had to thank for that; it was his mother's barrow he wanted to honour with a big stone. The Danes refused to obey – they revolted and deprived him of the kingdom. Harald's son Sven did not inherit Denmark – he was asked to take it by the Danes themselves! Thyre's efforts to make the royal power inheritable had only temporary success – but Valdemar and Absalon "finished with male genius the unfinished work of the brave woman" ...[89]

Kurt Johannesson has shown how critical Saxo is towards Valdemar's ideas about the hereditary succession.[90] Gesta Danorum opens with an election of a king, and Saxo thereby shows that the power to elect and dethrone kings has been in the hands of the people from time immemorial. It is true that Saxo maintains that certain families are more entitled to the royal dignity than others, but what the kings' sons could inherit was noble birth and the examples of their forefathers, worthy of imitation. "But then it is up to them in words and deeds to prove that they have inherited the virtues of their fathers too, and under forms established by juridical usage gain the assent of the people at the councils ("ting")."[91]

Saxo has probably written his story about Thyre on two levels in order to achieve the double aim of satisfying the opinion which cherished favourable ideas of Thyre (and "her" political plans), and to give his own picture, which corresponded to his other purposes:

By emphasizing Thyre's contributions to Denmark's defence Saxo displays Gorm's and Harald's unimportance, by emphasizing Thyre's cunning and calculation, he highlights Gorm's gullibility and weakness and gives us a further moral example of how "the female of the species is more deadly than the male". By emphasizing her ambition for rule Saxo can give us a warning example of the risks of hereditary royal power, illustrated by Harald's lack of ability, and how unfamiliar the Danes were/are with this new principle. It is probably not coincidental that Thyre and Valdemar are compared.

Saxo does not deny Thyre's great contribution to Denmark's defence, but he reduces it by giving it only small space in his history. Probably the thought that the Danes should have a woman to thank for their rescue must have appeared so disturbing and revolting to Saxo – and many others with him – that he had to interfere and tone down the far from glorious fact that a – foreign – woman had been called the "healer", "the honour" – and "the head" of the Danes.

By means of silence, insinuations and irony Saxo manages to carry through his different levels and alongside a more "traditional" picture of Thyre put forward his own.

How, finally, are Saxo's last words about Thyre to be explained? He writes:[92]

"Then Thyre, Denmark's head, died. Harald gave her a honourable funeral and buried her near his father's barrow; there was nobody who did not with his whole house partake in the mourning for this great loss: they believed that a private person's death had put an end to the communal prosperity of the whole country."

Saxo does not comment himself – he seems just to convey the reaction in Denmark after her death. But by the adjective "privato" Saxo points out that she was not the legal ruler of the Danes; she had had Denmark as her private property. By telling us how the Danes reacted after Thyre's death Saxo also illustrates how weak Harald must have been, and how little confidence the Danes had in him.

The reaction of the Danes corresponds to the reaction after Valdemar's death about 200 years later, when the fall of the country was believed to follow as a consequence. – But Valdemar's son Kanute had at his side Archbishop Absalon, who brought the war against the Vends to a successful end. Thyre's son Harald, however, had no support at home: he asked for help in Vendland against the Danes. During Sven's first period as king of Denmark there was no end to all the misfortunes, until he had taken the Christian faith. Now he found a man at his side who helped him and the Danes to success. It was Poppo, who christened the Danes and became their first bishop. – Saxo seems critical towards the indiscriminate confidence in a single person (a strong royal power?) that was cherished among his contemporaries. With his work Saxo clearly shows that "the Common Weal" of Denmark in the long run was based on – and demanded – more than the contributions of one single person. The pillars of society were, besides the king, the aristocracy – and the Church.

---

[1] For a modified and more detailed interpretation of Saxo's treatment of women, see the author's thesis *Kvinnor och män i Gesta Danorum*, Göteborg 1980 (Kvinnohistoriskt arkiv, 18). The following texts and translations have been used: SAXONIS *Gesta Danorum*. Rec. et ed. J. Olrik & H. Ræder, vol. 1, Copenhagen 1931 (abbreviated GD). The Sigrid episode is found GD 281,3-4 & 282,31-283,33. – SAKSES *Danesaga*. Oversat af Jørgen Olrik, 4 vols., København 1908-11 (abbreviated *Danesaga* I-IV). See *Danesaga* II,210 & 214-217. – *Heimskringla or the lives of the Norse kings by Snorre Sturlason*. Ed

with notes by Erling Monsen and transl. with the assistance of A.H. Smith, Cambridge 1932 (abbreviated H). See H p. 110 & 149-151 & 163-165 & 184-186.

[2] GD 283,6-9: *Quo nuntio Olavus ad summam usque gratulationem evectus, matronali stolae illibatas pudicitiae faces praeferendas existimabat virgineumque adulatus amplexum adolescentiam suam intra viduitatis gremium obterere passus non est. Igitur, quantum alteri contemptus alterique venerationis deferret, aperuit.*

[3] GD 283,16-18: *Nec contenti nautae amplissimam maiestatem, ultimo dedecore confudisse, quo clarius libidinosum ei animum exprobrarent, inflicti casus turpitudinem clamore sub hinnitus specie edito prosecuti sunt.*

[4] GD 282,22-25: *At regina paene pelago praefocata magno cum Sueonum rubore aegre litori restituta est. Tandem, recepto spiritu, impudictiam sibi a rege exprobratam iudicans, ruborem periculi tacita ferre nequivit, opprobrii deformitatem minis, quibus potuit, insecuta.*

[5] H 165.

[6] H 185.

[7] H 185.

[8] LAURITZ WEIBULL, *Kritiska undersökningar i Nordens historia omkring år 1000,* København 1911, p. 122 (reprinted in his *Nordisk historia. Forskningar och undersökningar,* vol. 1, Lund 1948, pp. 245-360).

[9] *amplissimam maiestatem, ultimo dedecore;* for the quotation in extenso see note 3 above.

[10] *integerrimae maiestatis regina, ignominiae ludibrum;* for the quotation in extenso see GD 283,25-28.

[11] As for the Icelandic usage of dialogues compared with their non-existence in Saxo, PAUL HERRMANN comments *(Erläuterungen zu den ersten neun Büchern der dänischen Geschichte des Saxo Grammaticus,* vol. 2, Leipzig 1922, p. 37): "Die schlechthin meisterhafte, lebenswahre Kunst in der Gesprächführung der Isländer, die 'nicht schwatzt, sondern schlägt', konnte Saxo schon darum nicht widergeben, weil er, im Banne des Latein stehend, fast nur indirekte Rede gebraucht".

[12] H, Index: Gunhild "the King's mother".

[13] H, Index: Astrid "Olav's daughter" (esp. p. 476).

[14] H 638.

[15] H: Skjalv p. 13; Bera 14; Asa Ingjald's daughter 30-31; Asa Harald's daughter 34-36; Gudrun Iron-skeggi's daughter 171.

[16] GD 80,31-81,9; *Danesaga* I,154-156.

[17] GD 82,7-9 & 12, 82,39-83,8; *Danesaga* I,158 & 160.

[18] GD 116,8-20, 122,5-21; *Danesaga* I,225 & 226 & 237-238.

[19] GD 166,2-9 & 25-34, 167,1-2, 168,1-10 & 27, 169,22-24, 172,25-173,32, 174,12-14; *Danesaga* I,323-339.

[20] GD 196,27-197,24; *Danesaga* II,34-35.

[21] GD 231,3-31; *Danesaga* II,99-100.

[22] GD 233,36-234,25; *Danesaga* II,103-106.

[23] GD 374,18-23; *Danesaga* III,174-175.

[24] GD 388,39-389,2; *Danesaga* III,209.

[25] GD 531,30-36; *Danesaga* IV,272.

[26] GD 506,21-29; *Danesaga* IV,214.

[27] GD 52,35-53,8; *Danesaga* I,101.

[28] GD 122,7-8; *Danesaga* I,238.

[29] GD 157,28-161-14; *Danesaga* I,238.

[29] GD 157,28-161,14; *Danesaga* I,309-315.

[30] GD 70,5-72,12; *Danesaga* I,132-136.

[31] GD 92,1-13; *Danesaga* I,176.

[32] GD 92,9-13; *Danesaga* I,176.

[33] GD 334,4-18; *Danesaga* III,84-85.

[34] GD 27,5-9; *Danesaga* I,51.

[35] GD 48,8-12; *Danesaga* I,91-92.

[36] GD 197,25-40; *Danesaga* II,35-36.

[37] GD 48,30-50,23; *Danesaga* I,93-96.

[38] GD 200,18-19, 202,29-203,18, 205,3-206,26; *Danesaga* II,41 & 45-46 & 49-52.

[39] GD 214,24-26, 215,5-6, 218,20-21, 220,11-221,7; *Danesaga* II,67-68 & 74 & 78-80.

[40] GD 272,5-17; *Danesaga* II,190.

[41] GD 251,30-252,10, 253,21-254,6; *Danesaga* II, 146-148 & 150-151.

[42] GD 271,6-8; *Danesaga* II, 188.

[43] *Women warriors:* Saela GD 77,14-16 (*Danesaga* I,148); Rusla 102,5-7, 208,21-24, 222,37-223,24 (I,198, II,56 & 83-85); Stikla 135,28-29, 208,20-24 (I,264, II,56); Asmund's sister 207,7-23 (II,53); Alvild 190,31-192,10 (II,25-27); Gro 192,10 (II,27); Hede 214,24-26, 215,5-6, 218,20-21, 220,21-221,7 (II,67 & 74 & 78-80); Visna 214,24 & 30-31, 218,21-22, 219,3 (II,67-68 & 74-75); Vejborg 214,26, 219,10-12 (II,68 & 76); Ladgerd, see note 41.

[44] (Swanhvid) GD 39,23-42,9, 42,13-26, 48,8-10; *Danesaga* I,73-77 & 91-92.

[45] GD 104,25-26, 105,7-12, 108,1-7, 115,1-2,117,35-118,5, 118,16, 119,9-11 & 24-25, 120,14, 122,4 & 17-21, 125,24, 129,6; *Danesaga* I,203 & 210 & 223 & 229 & 237.

[46] *Danesaga*, Preface to III-IV pp. 36-37.

[47] KURT JOHANNESSON. *Saxo Grammaticus. Komposition och världsbild i Gesta Danorum*, Stockholm 1978 (Lychnos-Bibliotek, 31), pp. 69-78.

[48] JOHANNESSON p. 78.

[49] No account is here taken of NANNA DAMSHOLT. 'Women in Latin medieval literature in Denmark e.g. annals and chronicles', *Aspects of female existence. Proceedings from the St. Gertrud symposium "Women in the Middle Ages" Copenhagen, September 1978*. Ed. by Birte Carlé et al., Copenhagen 1980, pp. 58-68 (p. 64f. on Thyra), which appeared after this paper was submitted for publication.

[50] GD 267,32-34. For the English translation, see *The first nine books of the Danish history of Saxo Grammaticus*. Transl. by Oliver Elton, 2 vols., London 1905[2], vol. 2 p. 574 (abbr. Elton). If not otherwise stated the English translations are my own.

[51] GD 266,19-21: *Illa, ut erat gravitate atque industria ante alias praestans, condicionem proco attulit, non ante se ei nupturam praefata, quam Daniam sub dotis nomine recepisset. sub dotis nomine* is here interpreted as "morning-gift"; the translation "home-gift" is impossible in the context. See also HERRMANN op.cit. vol. 1, Leipzig 1901, p. 431 note 1, and *Danesaga* II,178.

[52] GD 266,29-30. For the English translation, see SAXO GRAMMATICUS. *The history of the Danes. Books I-IX*. Transl. by Peter Fisher. Ed. with a commentary by Hilda Ellis Davidson, vol. 1, Cambridge 1979, p. 295 (abbr. Fisher).

[53] GD 266,31-34, English: Fisher 295.

[54] GD 267,15-16, English: Fisher 296.

[55] GD 271,30.

[56] GD 272,12-14: *Siquidem priori munitione fundamenti loco usi, imperfectum femineae virtutis propositum virili prudentia compleverunt, tanto excellentius opus edentes, quanto se muliebri noverant industria clariores.*

[57] GD 272,14-17: *Eadem quoque, cum sub specie feminae virilem animum gereret, Scaniam*

Suetica dominatione compressam praestandi tributi onere liberavit. Itaque hinc muro, inde armis hostem repellens, diversis patriae finibus par tutelae beneficium peperit.

[58] As to the discussion (opened by Hans Brix 1927) whether the apposition is to be related to Thyre or Gorm, see LAURITZ WEIBULL, 'Tyre Danmarkar bot' (*Scandia* vol. 1 (1928) pp. 187-202, reprinted in:), *Nordisk historia* ... (cf. above note 8), vol. 1 pp. 225-243 (esp. pp. 234-243).

[59] LAURITZ WEIBULL, 'Godfreds och Tyre Danebods Danevirke' *(Historisk tidsskrift för Skåneland* vol. 4 (1910-13) pp. 374-388, reprinted in:), *Nordisk historia* ..., vol. 1 pp. 209-223; see p. 219.

[60] Ibid. p. 220.

[61] WEIBULL, 'Tyre Danmarkar bot' pp. 228-231.

[62] As to the suggestions of two different building periods (discarded by L. Weibull) see WEIBULL, 'Godfreds...' p. 218 and 238.

[63] WEIBULL, 'Tyre ...' pp. 230-231.

[64] Ibid. p. 243. See also ERIK KROMAN, *Det danske Rige i den ældre Vikingetid*, København 1976, pp. 112-114.

[65] WEIBULL, *Kritiska undersökningar* ... (cf. above note 8) pp. 249-257.

[66] SVEN AGGESØN, *Kortfattet Historie om Danmarks Konger*. Paa Grundlag af M.Cl. Gertz' Tekstfremstilling og i Oversættelse ved Paul Læssøe Müller, København 1944, pp. 19-26.

[67] SVEN AGGESØN p. 19.

[68] Ibid. p. 25.

[69] Ibid. p. 26.

[70] WEIBULL, 'Tyre ...' p. 229.

[71] Ibid. pp. 222f. and 229f.

[72] WEIBULL, 'Godfreds ...' p. 221.

[73] WEIBULL, *Kritiska undersökningar* ... p. 253.

[74] See note 56 above.

[75] GD 266,26-29: *Itaque simulatione continentiae matrimonii experientiam interpellabat, cognoscendae posteritatis propositum pudicitiae specie colorando, commerciumque libidinis distulit, verecundiae figmento fortunam propagandae successionis explorans.* English: Elton vol. 2 p. 573.

[76] GD 267,13-16, English: Fisher p. 296.

[77] GD 267,18-19: *Itaque ut vafro, ita inusitato consilio pudicitiae simulatio in futurae prolis agnitionem transivit,* English: Fisher p. 296.

[78] STIG IUUL, *Fællig og Hovedlod. Studier over Formueforholdet mellem Ægtefæller i Tiden før Christian V's Danske Lov*, København 1940, p. 192.

[79] Ibid. p. 194.

[80] LIZZIE CARLSSON, *Jag giver dig min dotter. Trolovning och äktenskap i den svenska kvinnans äldre historia*, 2 vols., Stockholm 1965-72 (Skrifter utg. av Institutet för rättshistorisk forskning. Ser. 1. Rättshistoriskt bibliotek, 8 & 20), vol. 1. p. 210.

[81] Ibid. p. 212. See also HANS PETERSSON, *Morgongåvoinstitutet i Sverige under tiden fram till omkring 1734 års lag*, Stockholm 1973 (Skrifter utg. av Institutet för rättshistorisk forskning. Ser. 1. Rättshistoriskt bibliotek, 21), e.g. pp. 29, 61, and 433.

[82] Elton vol. 1 p. 59.

[83] CARLSSON vol. 2 p. 29.

[84] GD 267,5-12, English: Fisher p. 296.

[85] GD 267,16-18: *... continentis animi virtutem admissi concubitus satietate pensando, praefata minime se ei nupturam fuisse, nisi ex his adumbratae quietis imaginibus certiorem fecunditatis suae fortunam hausisset.*

[86] GD 268,27-28: *Quo dicto marito mortem, sibi ˈˈiduitatis causam praebuit nec ante filium quam coniugem planxit.*

[87] GD 268,25-27.

[88] GD 269,2: *hereditariae dominationis.*

[89] See note 56 above.

[90] JOHANNESSON (see note 47 above) p. 315ff. (Hitherto Saxo has been considered to advocate hereditary succession, just like Sven Aggesen. Cf. e.g. AKSEL E. CHRISTENSEN, *Kongemagt og aristokrati. Epoker i middelalderlig dansk statsopfattelse indtil unionstiden,* København 1945, pp. 41-44).

[91] Ibid. p. 316.

[92] GD 274,17-22: *Post haec Thyra, Danicae maiestatis caput, absumpta est. Cuius corpus Haraldus amplissimo funere elatum magno cum omnium plangore non longe a patris tumulo sepulturae mandavit. Neque enim tam acri iactura cuiusquam penates maeroris expertes esse poterant; privato funere publicam patriae fortunam exspirasse credentes. Ubi nunc quoque sacrarium perspicere est, duorum coniugum socialibus bustis intersitum.*

INDEX